Filming the Impossible

Travels in Search of Adventure
LEO DICKINSON

JONATHAN CAPE
THIRTY-TWO BEDFORD SQUARE LONDON

To My Mother

frontispiece: Filming over Pope Valley, California
1   White-out on the Patagonian Ice Cap

First published 1982
Paperback edition 1986
Introduction copyright © 1982 by Audrey Salkeld
Text copyright © 1982 by Leo Dickinson
Illustrations copyright © as stated in the Acknowledgments
Jonathan Cape Ltd, 32 Bedford Square, London WC1B 3EL

British Library Cataloguing in Publication Data
Dickinson, Leo
   Filming the impossible: travels in search of adventure.
   1. Dickinson, Leo   2. Photographers – England –
   Biography
   I. Title
   770'.92'4   TR140.D/
   ISBN 0 224 02015 3 (hardback)
   ISBN 0 224 02392 6 (paperback)

Set in Monophoto Bembo by Keyspools Ltd, Golborne, Warrington
Printed in Italy by New Interlitho, SpA, Milan

CONTENTS

INTRODUCTION

FOR THE PAST TWELVE YEARS Leo Dickinson has travelled the world photographing adventure as it happened. There can be few who have not seen one of his films on television, even if his name is not immediately familiar. It is only necessary to mention that he is the one who made the documentaries on climbing Everest without oxygen, or canoeing down the bubbling waters of the Dudh Kosi, river of Everest, for the connection to register. His films have been shown in over twenty countries and have collected as many awards, including the coveted Grand Prix at the 1978 Paris Film Festival. And for all those that resulted from his own initiative, energy and close attention to the practical realities, there have been as many for which he was sought out with invitations from the world's leading adventurers who had come to recognise his special talent.

Not that camera technique and an eye for drama are the only skills that have made Leo Dickinson one of the most accomplished film-makers in the field. Being the sort of person who instinctively eschews publicity for himself yet inspires confidence and friendliness in others, he tends to find himself at the centre of any project or expedition he is engaged upon and able therefore to communicate to audiences in subtle ways the spirit that moves behind the physical and mental ordeals undertaken by those who test themselves to the limit in the remotest parts of the world.

People often ask him which came first, his interest in photography or his passion for climbing. In fact they both date back to the year he was fourteen and borrowed his mother's Kodak Retinette for an excursion to the Lake District. Around this time he discovered that his school had a darkroom which was hardly ever used, and immediately disappeared into it. For hours, or indeed days on end, he would skip classes, lock himself away and live in a world of his own. Weekends were spent rock-climbing, often in North Wales, where he had undergone his initiation, bivouacking for a bitter January week in Snowdonia in the worst winter in living memory, when even Llyn Idwal froze to a foot in depth.

In 1966 he ventured on his first alpine season in the Dolomites. What he lacked in height and physique he overcame with inventiveness. Following up behind a lanky six-foot mountaineer from Colorado, Layton Kor, who is possessed of enormous reach, he found that pegs had been inserted more than two feet beyond his grasp. He quickly perfected a technique of lassoing them.

2 Prepared to film parachuting at night

Leo Dickinson left Blackpool School of Art in 1968 with both second-
and third-year prizes for photography. Having absorbed theory and
technique, he spent a year living by selling his architectural and climbing
pictures. But it soon became apparent to him that there would be more
scope for creative self-expression in movies. Not short on ambition or
confidence, he decided that his first film would be nothing less than a first-
hand view of climbing the North Face of the Eiger. Despite his lack of
experience, there was something about his infectious optimism that
persuaded Yorkshire Television to back him. They were not disappointed. Where other cameramen had failed, he succeeded with a team of
three other climbers in scaling the Eiger's vicious North Wall and
bringing back the first ever film of this notoriously dangerous climb.

The achievement was the more remarkable for the unusual quality of
that film. Far from being just a collection of associated incidents, it was a
fluent story which captured the full drama of the ascent and involved the
viewer in its wildness and isolation. It is easy to forget how much the
cameraman has to attend to besides the rigours of the climb. Whatever the
hazards, he must detach one part of his mind in order to maintain an
objective overall view, and at the same time manipulate the camera
controls and continually search for the most telling composition in his
viewfinder.

Of course one cannot plan in advance the storyline for a documentary
adventure film, but it is possible to imagine some of the likely outcomes
and devise beforehand means by which they may best be captured on film.
Leo has a flair for this sort of visualisation. He never tires of working out
new camera angles, new positions where a camera might be placed –
attached to a climber's arm or a skier's leg, at the water-line on the front of
a canoe, suspended below a balloon basket to trail in the waters of the Nile
and perhaps record snapping crocodiles... Even so, it is impossible to
forecast exactly what will happen, and in the end there is no substitute for
the almost intuitive alertness to those moments of unexpected poignancy
that so characterise a Leo Dickinson film.

I have often wondered how television film departments respond to
the long lists of camera adaptations they receive from Leo Dickinson
before each new expedition. Requests to provide heatproof or watertight
cameras, with time-lapse and ultrasonic controls and all manner of
electronic gadgetry; to make them light-weight by drilling away all
surplus metal; for tripods to support them horizontally rather than
upright – all these must pose the technicians as much of a challenge as the

3   Nearing the Mittelegi Ridge on the Eiger

expedition's own stated objective. Yet such close attention to detail in the preparation stages pays off in the field. Few who have seen it will forget the canoeists'-eye view of turbulent river water, or the horizon turning full circle as the cameraman somersaults out of a balloon basket.

After climbing, Leo branched out into other adventure sports. His head for heights was to prove a useful legacy there too. In situations that look crazily perilous to most people – dangling from balloons or helicopters, or strung in a taut skein of ropes across a precipitous gorge – he is able calmly to carry on filming in what he likes to call 'completely controlled circumstances'. When invited to film a ballooning expedition over the Sahara, he decided he would need to get *out*side the basket in order to secure really exciting footage. A proficiency in parachuting seemed to be the answer. So he spent a year, largely in the United States, cramming into every waking hour as many parachute jumps as possible. Not once did he allow his application to flag, even when faced with such setbacks as broken bones or a malfunctioning parachute. Indeed, before long, he was completely hooked on his new sport and eager to explore its latest expression, Canopy Relative Work. Within a couple of years of being a complete novice, he was taking part in world-record formations. It is this total commitment that Leo Dickinson is somehow able to convey through his camera, thus involving viewers in activities many of them are never likely to experience for themselves first-hand.

Most of the decade of high adventure that is recounted in this thrilling, sometimes funny, often moving book was undertaken with the help and support of the Welsh climber Eric Jones, who himself became the solo performer in one nerve-racking episode. The elder by ten years, Eric was about to make a solo attempt on the Bonatti Pillar on the Dru when the two men first met. Lumbering up behind, with Brian Molyneaux on his rope, Leo was horrified by the sight of the tall, quiet Welshman with little or no protection nimbly moving above them from one precarious stance to another. They found him on one ledge, resting, calm but pale and clearly shaken. He had fallen off a rock wall some little way up ahead. Normally solo climbers only ever fall once. Unroped, they have no one to check their downward progress. Eric Jones had been lucky not to plunge to his death. Peeling off the rockface he had grabbed his étrier (a little three-rung ladder) which had been left hooked to a piton a few feet below on the end of a thin piece of nylon line attached to his waist so that he could be pulled up after him. Though never intended to be strong enough to hold his weight, it checked the climber's fall and supported him long enough to regain a foothold.

Despite the narrowness of the escape, there was no persuading the

Welshman to abandon his solo attempt and join the roped pair. All the same, a lasting friendship had been formed. Working together in complete harmony – Leo providing the drive and enthusiasm, Eric the solid ground-sense and experience – they were to become an unassailable team. It was a combination almost bound to break the Eiger's repeated denial to all previous film attempts. As indeed it was again, almost ten years later, to provide a spectacular film record of the first successful British solo ascent of the same infamous rockface.

Inevitably, the question arises as to what it is that makes anyone want to go off and do so many dangerous things, repeatedly putting life at risk. Equally, it is perhaps natural for there to be no ready answer to the quandary posed by the lifestyle of such as Leo Dickinson, or of those whose exploits he brings to our firesides. To say that filming life-or-death adventure is fun, a game, a way of seeing the world in its most beautiful and most awful guises, seems altogether too glib a response. But that is about all one can get from Leo Dickinson, who simply does not see the need for any excuse for what he loves doing most. No one talks of the possibility of dying. And few ever give up, having faced the worst. You could call it an act of faith.

Like most adventurers, Leo Dickinson is a compulsive doer. Inactivity comes hard to him. After only a few minutes in a chair he becomes restless, needing constantly the stimulation of new faces, new challenges, new problems to solve pragmatically. Although in many ways a private person, he is generous and warm-hearted, with a rare knack of making people feel that much more is possible than ever they had dared to hope. It is perhaps in this sense that he comes closest to resolving the conundrum of his time spent filming what most of us usually prefer to regard as the impossible.

Clevedon
November 1981

AUDREY SALKELD
Fellow of the Royal Geographical Society

I
THE GREAT BALLOON RACE

Sunward I've climbed, and joined the
tumbling mirth/Of sun-split clouds – and
done a hundred things/You have not
dreamed of – wheeled and soared and
swung/High in the sun-lit silence.
John Gillespie Magee

IN JULY 1978 a Scottish engineer set off from St John's in Newfoundland on what he hoped would be the first successful manned balloon flight across the Atlantic. After travelling 1,999 miles, Don Cameron and Chris Davey, his co-pilot, were forced down in the sea only 110 miles from the Brittany coast.

It was about a hundred years since the first trans-Atlantic attempt had been made yet, within two weeks, Cameron was to see an American crew snatch the honour from him by making it all the way to France. After that, a non-stop round-the-world flight by manned balloon came to be considered the last great adventure, the Everest of aeronautics. Success would rank with the conquest of the Poles or the first four-minute mile. It would be a tremendous human achievement against prodigious odds.

Don Cameron, who was the first to cross the Alps in a hot-air balloon, and who earns a living making balloons in a converted church hall in Bristol, was not going to let another great prize slip from his grasp. Rising to the new challenge, he began to sketch out plans for a massive helium/hot-air combination balloon capable of hoisting aloft a fifteen-foot gondola, which would in fact be a pressurised cabin, a self-contained life-support system for four men. The idea was to get into one of the jet-streams that encircle the earth above 30,000 feet and be blown, literally, round the world in a matter of days. No one had yet attempted such an ambitious feat.

4   *opposite:* Well tied down to prevent premature take-off
5   *above:* Pouring out sand to gain altitude for my experiment in Don Cameron's baby helium balloon

By 1980, two of the successful Atlantic first-fliers, Maxie Anderson and Ben Abruzzo, having gone their separate ways, had each declared himself a candidate for the last great ballooning prize. Others were soon to follow. It was fast turning into an international race. But there was still a great deal of work to be done before anyone could take off.

From the outset the project was beset by difficulties – first financial, then technical, and finally political. The biggest problem to be overcome was finding a power source capable of maintaining a life-supporting pressure system. Above 30,000 feet atmospheric pressure falls to less than half the 14.7 lb per square inch that it is at sea-level; at 40,000 feet it is almost down to a quarter. High-flying jet aircraft have power in abundance, bled off their engines, with which to maintain pressurised cabins. A balloon travelling at only the speed of the prevailing wind cannot command the luxury afforded by air being rammed into turbines at the airspeed of a Boeing or a Concorde.

Ahead lay months of testing materials, developing prototypes, and ensuring the seaworthiness of the gondola. If nothing else, at least it was settled that Don, as Chief Pilot, would be joined on the flight by two other experienced balloonists, and I would accompany them as flight cameraman to make a film for ATV. It seemed sensible, therefore, that I should get in some high-altitude experience. Why not, I suggested to Richard Creasey at ATV, make an attempt on the balloon world altitude record?

Though men have dreamed of flying since the time of the Greeks (indeed Leonardo da Vinci has left us his drawings from the fifteenth century of an aeronautically sound flying machine), it was not until 1783 that all the practical difficulties were overcome. In June that year, two Frenchmen, Étienne and Joseph Montgolfier, papermakers by trade, decided to test the notion that heated air and smoke, trapped in a bag, would be sufficient to raise a body into the air. The gas which was to lift their linen and paper balloon to a height of 500 feet was made by burning moist straw and wood on an iron platform just below the opening to the inverted bag. The hot-air balloon was born.

Later that year, in the French capital, the physicist Professor Charles constructed a spherical balloon of varnished silk which he inflated with hydrogen, then a newly-discovered gas, lighter than air but extremely volatile and not inexpensive. Before a huge crowd of spectators, it rose from the Champ de Mars and gently descended half an hour later in a field fifteen miles away, where a frightened crowd attacked it with farm implements, believing it to be a monstrous bird which gave off an evil smell when its skin was pierced. The French Government thought the time had come to send out a proclamation to reassure people who were clearly alarmed by the sudden influx of flying machines.

Not to be outdone by their new rival, the Montgolfiers demonstrated their hot-air balloon before the King at Versailles with some farm animals in a cage attached to it, and then agreed to allow a French professor, Pilâtre de Rozier, to go up suspended beneath the hot-air balloon. Just to show that his first brief flight had been no mere fluke, de Rozier went up again, accompanied this time by the Marquis d'Arlandes, and, despite inadvertently setting the balloon fabric alight, accomplished safely a five-and-a-half-mile journey to the outskirts of the city.

Momentarily forgotten in the excitement over de Rozier's first manned flight, Professor Charles prepared an even more spectacular event with which to close that historic year in aviation. In an opulently decked out, not to say gaudily colourful balloon, with a gold-braided basket suspended below full of all manner of instruments, a valve fitted at the top and worked by a cord from below to allow gas to escape when descent was required, sand-bags as ballast in the basket, Charles flew with his friend Robert the twenty-seven miles from Paris to Nesle in two hours. Whereupon, Robert left the balloon, leaving Charles recklessly careering off again to a height approaching 12,000 feet.

6   Death of an Aeronaut   7   A Terrible Moment

Despite a Channel crossing and many other achievements in the new flying craze, ballooning remained altogether too expensive a pursuit for more than a very few of the well-to-do to indulge. In 1846 a Frenchman by the name of Arban flew alone in a hydrogen balloon across the Alps, peering down in the intense cold through the storm that accompanied him for most of the way at precipices of snow and ice no mortal eye had beheld before and no human foot trod. But the most astonishing flight of the century was, to my mind, that of 1862, one of a series of eight scientific flights made on behalf of the British Association.

The veteran balloonist Henry Coxwell conducted very thorough preparations before taking aloft a scientist by the name of Glaisher. On 5 September all was ready, and the two men made a rapid ascent from Wolverhampton in the early afternoon. Innumerable instruments were set out neatly on a table installed in the open wicker basket that formed the gondola. In half an hour they had gained a height of four miles, or well over 20,000 feet.

However, something was going seriously wrong. They were gaining too much height, too rapidly. While occupied with his observations and instrument readings, Glaisher began to notice an impairment of his sight. As they approached the five-mile altitude, he attempted to write down some notes, only to find his right arm useless. His left arm worked no better, and soon he felt unable to hold up his head, or even to speak. For a short while, his mind remained alert while his body slumped back, helpless. Then he lost all consciousness.

Coxwell, meanwhile, had clambered out of the basket in an attempt to free the entangled valve line in the ring above – by no means an easy task, as hoar frost had begun to gather round the neck of the balloon in the intense cold. His hands frozen, Coxwell dropped back to find Glaisher insensible in the bottom of the basket. By now, he too was losing control of his limbs. Without speedy action, they would not get down alive. Seizing the valve line in his teeth, Coxwell tugged frantically with his head. Slowly the balloon began to descend and Glaisher resumed his place at the table as if nothing worse had happened than that he had dozed off momentarily. Landing in a remote spot, with no one about, the two men walked the seven miles into Ludlow. From careful calculation, Glaisher put their maximum height at 37,000 feet. It was a record that was to stand unbeaten until well into the next century.

The British balloonist Julian Nott took a hot-air balloon to a height of 45,850 feet in India in 1974, and this stood as a world record until Chauncey Dunn, an American, pushed it up to 53,200 feet in 1979. Dunn almost killed himself in the process. He had travelled in an unpressurised gondola and suffered from a high-altitude version of diver's bends. Ed Yost, the father of modern hot-air ballooning, explained to me that at 53,000 feet, without oxygen or pressure-suit, it would take less than twenty seconds for the blood to boil. There, ten miles above the earth's surface, the temperature can drop to −92°F. The summit of Everest seemed positively cosy by comparison.

'How high can a hot-air balloon go?' I asked Yost.

'No one knows,' he said. 'But it sure scares me . . . and I'm fearless.'

With the promise of a film of his new attempt and sponsorship from ICI, Julian Nott set out to regain the height record at Albuquerque in New Mexico in October 1980. The world's biggest hot-air balloon meet was being held there that summer, and four hundred extravagantly decorated balloons lifting gently off the ground at once promised a fittingly spectacular backdrop. Julian hoped to get up to 60,000 feet. My plan was to go with him halfway, then jump out – with parachute, of course, and a ten-minute supply of oxygen – filming as I went.

Unlike such anarchic pastimes as mountaineering and canoeing, ballooning is bound by bureaucracy. No records are now recognised unless you play strictly by the rules. Not wishing to put at risk Julian's attempt to break the record, I urged that we should get official clearance for what we proposed. A telex was duly dispatched to the Federal Aeronautical Institution asking if my parachuting out of the balloon during the flight in any way breached the rules. The necessary clearance came by return:

Only items specified in Para 4.9,20F Section 10F the code must not be jettisoned. As the passenger does not fly the balloon I suppose he may be considered as ballast. No offence. Regards

R. Pat Welsh NATAERO. 64149.

So, ballast I was. That was fine by me.

Though the warm red sands and tumbleweed bushes of New Mexico offered attractive scenery for a film, there were to be unforeseen snags. During the week we spent in Albuquerque the wind never once dropped sufficiently to enable us to launch a balloon as large as our ICI monster, *Innovation*. Most hot-air balloons are a sixth of the size of ours, and calm take-off conditions are considered essential even for them.

Always supposing we could eventually get airborne, the wind threatened to carry us some distance from the launch-site, portending all sorts of possible catastrophes. If, for instance, we came down in the Navajo Reservation, we could say goodbye to the balloon – and maybe

8   *overleaf:* Balloons over Albuquerque

the parachutist as well – since by law, the Indians are allowed to keep any property passing through (and presumably dropping into) their hunting grounds. Quite a lot of tepees could be cut from a 375,000-cubic-foot balloon, but as my parachute would presumably only make half a tepee, it was more than likely that I would finish up married off to their ugliest squaw! South of Albuquerque lay a huge laser factory; to stray unawares across a laser beam would mean sterilisation at the very least. Measured against arrows and lasers, rattlesnakes (abundant in these parts) seemed almost innocuous.

Altogether it added up to the fact that we were in the wrong place. Eventually, at the invitation of Bob Kenny from Denver, the whole entourage moved to Colorado, where ten days later we were still glueing bits of balloon together, tightening various bolts and finishing off the hundred and one jobs that had to be done to get this huge contraption, weighing 1,400 lb, up in the air, with Julian and myself aboard.

I had planned several interesting camera angles to record events, and had taken precautions against the insidious cold by wrapping all the cameras in three inches of foam rubber and tape. The batteries were kept warm by being threaded into two Thermos flasks. Two cameras were suspended on long lines from the widest point of the balloon and, with wide-angle lenses, these promised not to let events escape them.

The gondola had a perspex dome on top, which was hinged to allow access. Should it fail to open in an emergency, a cord of plastic explosive taped all the way round, with a clearly marked red firing-pin, would provide an emergency exit. Twelve bottles of propane gas, one bottle of hydrogen, a huge bottle of pure oxygen and then this high-explosive charge – to me, in my innocence – all seemed to add up to a potentially enormous bang! And as if this wasn't enough, the burner system had to be ignited with a spark plug from a jet fighter. Jumping out of this balloon was going to be eminently more sane than staying aboard.

Prior to the flight, Julian had to breathe pure oxygen for thirty minutes to cleanse his body of any nitrogen, which would give him altitude bends. The count-down went without incident and we lifted gently off, so gently in fact that I didn't immediately realise we were airborne. Seen in our goggles, through the dome, we must have looked like two goldfish gaping out of an inverted bowl.

9   *opposite above:* Inside the high-altitude envelope
10   *below left:* Shortly before take-off in the baby helium balloon
11   *below right:* Checking the cameras that were to be suspended from the edge of the balloon on a thin nylon line
12   *overleaf, main picture:* Preparing to leave Julian Nott's high-altitude balloon at 15,000 feet
13   *inset:* Moment of departure

Anticipating that it would be pretty cold five miles up, I had dressed in my insulated mountaineering clothes. But the heat inside the dome was stifling, and I soon felt like stripping off. If the gondola had been painted black, Julian would have toasted at high altitude; if white, he would have frozen. The compromise was a deep blue which seemed in harmony with my feelings at that moment. When we reached 12,000 feet, Julian thoughtfully suggested we might open the dome to cool down.

A thick cloud layer had settled over Colorado that morning at 18,000 feet. While Denver Air Traffic Control accepted that they could keep track of an object as large as Julian's balloon, they were equally sure they would lose me from their screens, free-falling through the air lanes. I was happy to take my chance, avoiding the jumbos, even if my goggles misted over in the heavy cloud. But Denver was not prepared to allow me any such option. I was to bale out at around 15,000 feet, before we went into the cloud.

Obediently I clambered out of the gondola at the appointed time, switched on the cameras, gave a thumbs-up sign to wish Julian well, and leapt off backwards into space.

There is not much to do when you are falling from a great height. Time slows down and the earth doesn't seem to get any nearer, despite approaching at the rate of 1,000 feet every five seconds. You really have to make an effort to stop your mind wandering. I concentrated on keeping a wary eye out for any of those stray jets the Air Traffic people seemed so worried about.

I opened the parachute when I had got down to 3,000 feet, and then removed the claustrophobic oxygen mask and goggles. I peered round for a suitable landing spot and touched down in a little field at the side of a farm. As I started to gather in my parachute, a little silver-haired lady wandered over.

'I been livin' here forty year,' she exclaimed in a lovely mid-West drawl, 'and I never did see anythin' like you before!'

Julian's balloon had disappeared into the cloud layer and it was difficult to explain where I had come from. Assuring her that I was not an off-course astronaut, I suggested that she might like to switch on her radio and tune in to the local station to hear the latest progress on our flight. Yet, whether I had come from the moon or not, she wasn't going to pass up the opportunity of giving me a lavish breakfast.

High overhead, Julian's burner went out at 53,000 feet. With liquid propane gushing everywhere he could not relight the flame. The balloon had enough momentum to coast upwards to just above the 3 per cent margin required to set a new record over an old. Later, however, the

Federal Aeronautical Institution changed its mind and, despite their telex, decided that my jump invalidated Julian's ascent record. By dropping out, I had dropped Julian into a whole load of trouble, although the new record was recognised by the august Royal Aeronautical Club back home in Britain.

Meanwhile Don Cameron had produced a scaled-down version of the million-cubic-foot balloon he planned to build for the round-the-world attempt. It was a combination helium/hot-air balloon, and to inflate just this 'baby' (a mere 15,000 cubic feet) would have cost us 1,500 dollars. Fortunately, Air Products offered to let us have the precious helium free, provided we used it in the United States, where it can be tapped off from the wellheads in Kansas.

Combination balloons were invented by Pilâtre de Rozier almost 200 years ago, and even today such constructions are known as Rozier balloons. De Rozier was way ahead of his time, perhaps too far ahead, for his first and only combination balloon, in which he hoped to cross the English Channel, used highly inflammable hydrogen. All went well until he used the flame to create hot air. It proved the end of his expedition, the balloon and de Rozier. Not for nothing was 'Inflammable Air' the early name given to hydrogen. The helium we use today, unlike hydrogen, is an inert gas that does not form an explosive mixture.

Don's new balloon was made of 'Melinex', a polyester film only twelve microns thick laminated on to one-and-a-half-ounce ripstop nylon, which needed to be tested to see how well it would hold helium without leaking.

It was already November and the ground was covered with snow. Four flights were enough to satisfy Don that the material, design and construction would perform as he wished. But he still had one more test up his sleeve. He wanted to know if, in an emergency, the balloon envelope could be relied on to act as a parachute and bring the balloonists safely back to earth. Supposing helium were to be lost due to a split in the envelope, could the lower part of the balloon be cut free, allowing it to be sucked up inside against the top surface, so creating an enormous parachute? That was what he felt ought to happen.

The guinea pig to put it to the test was to be me. I was to make a solo flight in this baby-size balloon to see what would really happen.

Before setting off, I fixed one camera, aimed downwards, to the widest part of the balloon, then taped another to the inside of one of the four struts holding the basket. I also wore a helmet-mounted camera – as well, of course, as my parachute, just in case Don's theory was wrong.

Several sandbags were loaded aboard and the propane gas cylinder removed for safety. A VHF radio was installed so that Don could give me last-minute instructions. It all seemed fairly straightforward, even though I had never piloted a helium balloon before. If I threw out sand, I would go up; if I didn't, I would come down.

I wanted to take the balloon up to 12,000 feet, to give me a good margin of safety. With tremendous enthusiasm I started chucking out sand and the balloon shot up like a rocket. The variometer (which registers the rate of ascent or descent) showed a climb of 1,500 feet a minute! It did not occur to me that the balloon was in imminent danger of splitting. I just wanted to get to my 12,000 feet as quickly as possible. Some minutes later and six miles down-wind of my take-off point, I reached the required altitude and switched on my helmet camera.

There were two things I had to do to transform the balloon into a parachute: cut the lines holding the skirt round the bottom of the balloon with my Swiss army knife, and then pull open the valve at the top to allow helium to escape. With one last check that there was a large area free of obstructions for landing, I went ahead.

Sure enough, as the helium escaped, the lower part of the Rozier balloon was sucked up inside. It now looked like a pulsating jellyfish. For twenty seconds or so, everything worked according to plan and the balloon indeed became a parachute. Soon, however, it started to rotate, slowly at first but with gathering momentum. Another thirty seconds and it was no longer behaving anything like a parachute. It had become completely unstable and highly dangerous, like some huge beast thrashing about in its death-throes. The basket was being dragged round the sky sideways, spinning dizzily. It was time to abort the experiment and get the hell out of this contraption. I had just time enough to switch on the other cameras, still attached to the balloon, before grabbing the mike and screaming into it that I was baling out.

Getting away proved far from easy. The wires attaching the balloon to the basket were slackening and tightening in rapid spasm, but with no apparent pattern. If I fell through those wires, it would take a miracle to escape cleanly. It seemed more than likely that the camera on my helmet would get caught up in the lines and I should very likely hang myself.

I am not surprised that those on the ground noticed my voice rise an octave or two, for my predicament was compounded by another unforeseen difficulty – doing battle with the tremendous G-factor. I understand now why it is so difficult to get out of a stricken aircraft.

14   Strange distorted shapes appeared in the balloon fabric before it was completely filled

Climbing out on to the side of this basket was like negotiating the crux of an extremely hard rock climb in a hurricane. My body felt three times its normal weight and my arms weren't used to taking such strain. Luckily the forces changed for a moment and I was able to crawl down the side of the basket, but it was still like trying to climb out of one of the cars of a fairground whip while it is in full swing.

I didn't fall off; I was flung out and skidded across the sky, making three involuntary somersaults before stabilising enough to be able to open my chute. The sheer terror of it made me bite the mouth-switch off my camera so that I was unable to film my departure. Not that it mattered much as I was skittering sideways and didn't see balloon or basket again for some seconds. The camera tied to the edge of the balloon was still running, however, despite being whipped round the sky like a gaucho's bolas. It recorded me crawling along the top of the basket as I tried to extricate myself from the flailing wires and cords, and even from my Swiss penknife, which had acquired a life of its own, jerking and jabbing around dangerously in time with the basket's convulsions.

Once my parachute was fully open, I had to be careful to avoid the balloon as it fell past me. Within seconds it was level and I had the bizarre notion that I could walk along the top of it. But it was descending far too quickly for that. I chased it down by spiralling and spilling air from my parachute. But even dropping at 2,000 feet a minute, I could not catch that errant balloon.

It landed in a large open area with a heavy thud on the frozen ground. I came down next to it and quickly unclipped my parachute before going to investigate the two cameras. The film recovered from the wreckage was spectacular, some of the most condensed action I have ever been involved in, the balloon spinning against a snowy patchwork once every six seconds. Then I remembered that the camera was running in slow motion: the balloon, therefore, must have been revolving once every three seconds! A parachute in a tight spiral can rotate every couple of seconds, so it is easy to visualise the crazy speed of this wounded balloon.

Several minutes later Don Cameron and his team arrived, all looking relieved that I had survived the escapade, even if the theory of the balloon turning into a parachute had not worked out as expected. It was obvious that the balloon skirt, which I had cut free so as to allow it to fold up inside, had been forced back down again by pressurised air from the top, creating a sort of candle-balloon that was quite unstable. Most round parachutes have parts of the fabric removed to allow wind to spill out and so stabilise

15   Don Cameron (right) and Peter Bohanna (left) take off for an early-morning flight

16–19   After successfully getting the bottom half of the balloon to suck up inside the top, I was flung off the basket as it started gyrating rapidly

the descent, as well as to afford some steerage. This was lacking in our balloon, hence the violent ride. Without such vents, our full-size round-the-world balloon, with its 15,000 lb gondola slung below, if caught in a similar predicament, would probably shake us to pieces before we could abandon ship for a more conventional parachute descent.

Almost at once, Don began to talk of patching up his balloon, making a few modifications to the theory, and getting me to test it again. It was Thanksgiving Day in America. I was thankful just to be down on the

ground again, alive and in one piece. How did I manage to get into these crazy predicaments? By no means for the first time in the last ten years I had been rescued by fate from the very edge of disaster and I had no urge to tempt the gods again so soon. What interested me then was the idea of sampling that traditional ballooning ritual, the champagne breakfast. I suggested that we might ponder Don's proposition, slowly and carefully, over one such Thanksgiving breakfast.

It was not a question of drawing back from a potentially suicidal venture so much as the need for a breathing space in which to allow a measure of rational caution to enter into our calculations. After all, it had taken no less than twenty attempts before the Atlantic had been won. The first to set off round the world by balloon was far from guaranteed the prize of success.

As it happened, Maxie Anderson was to be the first away. His balloon, *Jules Verne*, rose into the sky over Egypt, his flight path heading for Iran and the promise that, should he violate Iranian air space, he would be shot down. Cautiously, in complete darkness, he managed to traverse the Ayatollah's ménage without being detected, only to spring a leak and be faced with no other choice than to abort the flight. He landed safely in India, on the Himalayan foothills, after little less than the longest ever balloon flight.

Anderson's Atlantic companion, Ben Abruzzo, was next away, from Japan. But, having miscalculated how long it would take to inflate so large a balloon, he missed his clear-weather window. He jettisoned his first envelope and ordered a second. No sooner was that in position than one of the retaining cables tore loose and, with several people hanging on, it took off, rising to a mere ten feet before crashing unceremoniously back to earth. Third time lucky. In November 1981 Ben Abruzzo made the first ever Pacific crossing, in eighty-four hours.

As I write, the last ballooning challenge remains, so to speak, up in the air! Yet with the Cameron enterprise back in the forefront of the race, who can say how it will all end? The question I am asked more often is how did it all begin; how did I embark on this strange life, journeying to the most inaccessible corners of the world, there to film the seemingly impossible feats of those who dare to challenge nature in her most awesome guises?

It was on a warm spring day in 1970 when, with precious little hard climbing experience and none at all as a professional movie-maker, I first summoned up the nerve to propose to Yorkshire Television a film that would be unique – if I managed to pull if off . . .

2

THE EIGER
EXPERIMENT

I have always regarded climbing as a
sophisticated escape – from artificiality to
reality.
Eric Shipton

THE NORTH FACE OF THE EIGER is not visible until you are almost into the
village of Grindelwald. As we rounded the bend that brings it into view, I
remember thinking that it didn't look as menacing as I had imagined.
Indeed it seemed almost to be reclining in the pastoral meadows. It took
only a few days to discover that this particular view is not the best,
conveying less than others the immense size and scale of this the greatest
mountain wall in Europe. It is only as you walk back from the little village
of Kleine Scheidegg, nestling at the Eiger's foot, and move towards
Mannlichen, that you get any impression of the Eiger's true stature.

The intricate classic route up the North Wall is over ten thousand feet in
length, and during its short history has claimed more lives – if not in fact,
then certainly in folklore – than any other mountain. In 1935 Max
Sedlmayer and Karl Mehringer were among the first to attempt the face.
They reached a point halfway up but lacked the technique necessary to get
them to the White Spider. After five nights on the wall, they perished in
their bivouac, which henceforth became known as Death Bivouac.
Already, with the deaths of the two Germans, the face had claimed four
lives, and the Eiger's legendary reputation was born. Most people
considered the North Face to be quite impossible, not least because it was
almost constantly bombarded with falling stones and ice. Six more men
died over the following two years and in 1938, Colonel Strutt, the retiring
President of the Alpine Club, in his farewell address, said, 'The
Eigerwand – still unscaled – continues to be an obsession for the mentally-

(left to right) Cliff, Pete and Eric at the Swallow's Nest

deranged of almost every nation. He who first succeeds may rest assured that he has accomplished the most imbecile variant since mountaineering first began.'

The Swiss Parliament passed a law forbidding attempts on the North Face, but it had to be revoked when seen to be impracticable to enforce. Finally, in 1938, two Austrians and two Germans became the first to succeed in scaling the Eiger's North Face, and so incidentally provided Hitler with valuable propaganda material for the prowess of blond Aryan heroes. The fact that none of the men – Anderl Heckmair, Heinrich Harrer, Fritz Kasparek or Ludwig Vörg – wanted any part of it was irrelevant. They were given a victors' welcome and were photographed with the Führer. Discretion, it seemed to them, was indeed the better part of valour.

After the Second World War, improved equipment and protective clothing led to more and more attempts on the Eigerwand. But still there was no easy way in which to brook the exhausting length of the climb or the treacherous weather, which is apt to change suddenly at half-hourly intervals. An ascent of the Eiger was still considered the ultimate measure of a climber's proficiency.

By 1969, 253 climbers had got to the top (78 of them during that one year), but so far no one had succeeded in filming the climb. Three times a German camera team had been turned back by appalling conditions. The problems involved in making such a film fascinated me; and besides, I wanted to see for myself what the Eiger really looked like and what it was about this mountain that attracted so much interest. Could I do any better than the German cameramen?

Even today, the route requires every ounce of skill and, above all, speed if one is to avoid the fatal accidents that await those who get stranded in sudden ferocious blizzards. I reckoned we would have to carry up to 200 lb of gear on our backs and take five to six days, crossing and recrossing some of the most dangerous traverses in order to get all the angles we needed for the film.

I had studied photography for three years at college and had the experience of four alpine climbing seasons. With no more than these credentials, I suggested the idea of an Eiger film to Tony Essex, then the Head of Documentaries at Yorkshire Television. Four months later, my team of four assembled, we were installed in a cowshed in Kleine Scheidegg, full of optimism, but smarting under the warnings, disbelief and discouragement of the local Jeremiahs who seemed to regard the

21   The central section of the Eiger North Wall, with the Second Icefield split by shadow, the Flatiron and Death Bivouac in the centre, and the immense chimney of the Ramp on the left. The Spider can be seen top centre.

Eiger as their own private death-trap. If you climbed it, you were a hero. If you failed – or died – you were incompetent. It seemed a harsh distinction.

Our credibility was not helped by our own brand of diplomacy. In those days, with the memory of Everest still fresh, British climbers felt they could out-climb anyone. We still held the lingering image of the continental guide who hauled up his clients while belayed to a finger of rock that would snap at the first jolt. We did not imagine standards had changed much since the days of Whymper, and took little account of the new generation of athletes who were beginning to 'run up' the hardest routes in the Alps.

I had discussed my Eiger plans first with Cliff Phillips, a year older than me at twenty-five. It was he who suggested that a team of four would be best. Eric Jones was his sometime climbing partner and Pete Minks was mine. The team was quickly selected. Cliff and Eric, it is true, climbed together frequently, but they rarely roped together. Both preferred to solo the very hardest routes without safety precautions. Pete Minks and I had a more sensible partnership; a majority of the climbs we had performed involved ropes.

One serious setback interrupted our preparations for the ascent. Cliff's natural affinity with the gods and his total disregard for gravity were cut down to size when he suffered a serious fall. With Eric Jones, he had been putting in a bit of training by mopping up some of the extreme routes on the north and south sides of Llanberis Pass which they had not done before. Cliff was soloing Blackfoot, which at that time had recorded few ascents and was regarded as a hard *Extremely Severe*. The crux was wet and he slipped off it, falling ninety feet before he hit a grassy ledge which catapulted him off into space. He span down to the screes another ninety feet below. Normally, a fall like this would be fatal. Indeed many have been killed on short ten-foot falls. Yet Cliff was lucky. He regained consciousness some minutes later and realised that, with no one about, he was also going to have to solo his own rescue! It took him half an hour to crawl down through the boulders to his van parked on the road. Somehow he got into the driving seat, and, with both wrists broken, a cracked pelvis, an inverted cheek bone, and heaven knows what other scrapes and bruises, he willed his vehicle down the road to the cottage where Eric was staying.

That Cliff had escaped so lightly was probably due to his slight, wiry build. He weighed only nine stone. All the same, his accident appeared to put paid to any idea of filming the Eiger in only a few weeks' time.

X-rayed and strapped up in hospital, Cliff was told he would be unable to climb for another six months. The rest of us began to think about a replacement, and this must have gone through Cliff's mind as well. Four days later he dressed and walked out of the hospital. Within ten days he was back on the rocks, soloing again, and in the space of six weeks he had completed the cycle from superfit, to a bad hospital case, and back to superfit again! Few would have had his determination.

In those days, Cliff was a strangely private person and it was not easy to get close to him. Even Eric, who had shared a lot of climbing experiences with him, found it hard to penetrate his shell. But if Cliff wanted something badly enough, he usually got it. He would simply direct his whole energies towards it. Several years later, he went back and soloed Blackfoot – this time without disastrous consequences. Unfinished plans and defeat were difficult for him to accept.

Eric Jones, at thirty-three the eldest of the team, was a taciturn Celt from North Wales. He had left an indelible impression on me the year before with his solo ascent of the Bonatti Pillar on the Dru, near Chamonix. At the time I was also on the route with Brian Molyneaux and was finding the climb hard. Without ropes, Eric seemed to be ambling upwards, completely calm and controlled. But he had one lucky escape when, halfway up, a piton pulled loose and left him dangling from a small 'fifi' hook, attached by a line to his waist. He regained his hold and completed the climb.

Pete Minks came from Liverpool and, in the tradition of the two most famous 'hard men' of the day, Joe Brown and Don Whillans, was a plumber. Together we had done many of the hardest climbs in Wales, with Pete leading the crucial passages, leaving me to immortalise him in photographs as best I could. Heavily built and very determined, he was, at twenty-three, the youngest of the team.

While waiting for the Eiger to come into condition, we decided to try an unclimbed rock pillar on the Italian side of Mont Blanc. Why the Central Pillar of Brouillard had not been attempted before was something of a mystery, and its light-grey granite slabs attracted us. We started at dawn after a warm dry bivouac in sleeping bags on the Brouillard Glacier. By early afternoon we were above the bergschrund at the foot of the Pillar, but we only managed to climb about four rope lengths before a storm was upon us. The weather had not been expected to break for at least another thirty-six hours and we were amazed at the speed with which it overtook us. We were unable to move up or down. That night I remember as a claustrophobic montage of suffocating 'black' snow pouring into the tent ceaselessly, intermingled with the odd, whistling

no one was to die on this trip. And it was some years before I matured enough to reason that the ultimate responsibility was mine and that, if someone died, I would question using the film. To me, then, falling climbers were there to be filmed, but a falling camera, that was something else. It would mean we had failed. A camera dropped from the Traverse of the Gods would fall 4,500 feet before hitting the First Pillar and ceasing to be a camera. Though I never did drop mine, I came close to throwing it once or twice.

On our next attempt, the Eiger changed tactics. Now the cameraman was to be the target for the mountain's wrath. We were at the bottom of the Second Icefield, with storm clouds all around us, as the stones began to fall. 'God's playing skittles with his disciples!' remarked Cliff. The boulder-strewn icefield was the skittle alley; *we* were the skittles. There, suddenly, we were subjected to an aerial bombardment. Cliff, poised beside Eric and me on a little scree-covered platform, continued to hurl insults at the heavens as the stones hurtled past. Pete, out ahead, began picking his way gingerly back towards us as, high above, another volley started. The rocks tumbled with spectacular grace, tracing a gentle but deadly parabolic path, before splattering on the rock around us. Pete swung off the ice on an old piece of frozen rope, left from an earlier ascent. I filmed, concentrating all my attention through the viewfinder, curiously oblivious to my own exposed position. I was immune, surely. Doesn't fate protect *all* cameramen in dangerous situations? I thought of war photographers in Vietnam, and then . . .

Seconds later I regained consciousness and became aware of a searing pain in my shoulder. Reassured of Pete's safety, I relapsed into misery, a misery compounded of pain, self-pity, a growing disinterest in the climb, and anger at our previous optimistic confidence. I wanted nothing more than to get off this evil mountain.

It took us a day and a half to make the descent, traversing the Japanese Route, bivouacking in a big wet cave, and then continuing wearily downwards. I had time to think, remember, and to revise my opinion of this Eiger, the Ogre.

When we reached the Hinterstoisser Traverse I paused to think of the German climber who had given his name to this slab of rock. He and his three companions had perished after reaching Death Bivouac in 1936. Hinterstoisser himself had fallen, two froze to death and the fourth, Toni Kurz, died dangling from a rope within feet of a rescue party. So far we had been lucky, but the long, macabre death-roll haunted me. The ghosts

23–5 Cliff Phillips losing his foothold and starting to tumble down the 200-feet-high snowfield

and memories of those past climbers – Brewster, Harlin, Kurz, Carruthers, Sedlmayer, Sandri, Hinterstoisser – kept eternal vigil with the swirling wind. It was indeed a pitiless and dangerous place. Were we to add our names to theirs?

The Eiger is a mile high from base to summit, but two miles by the zig-zagging route we were taking, the original 1938 Heckmair line which picks out its easiest passages. It is a mountain with a charisma few others can match. The names of its features are curiously romantic, as well as being household names around the world: Traverse of the Gods, Death Bivouac, Swallow's Nest and, most infamous of all, the White Spider.

Our first attempt had been doomed to failure from the start. We carried far too much equipment and it had been raining at the outset. Stones were washed down with repetitious harmony. Visibility was practically nil. But, most serious of all, we were mentally unprepared. As my shoulder healed, our determination strengthened until, finally, by early September, we were ready once more.

The famous Jungfrau Mountain Railway tunnels for miles through the very heart of the Eiger, and a little below the Difficult Crack there is a Gallery Window giving access on to the face. Having filmed the lower passages already, we decided to start our third attempt from this window. Still in darkness, we emerged through the hole on to the face at 4 am, bent low under our heavy packs. We were still below the Second Icefield from which we had retreated earlier, and, without any filming to hamper our progress, were initially able to make fast time. But the snow was much deeper than before and the conditions harder and colder. The Hinterstoisser had changed, and the weight of snow on the ropes had prised loose some of the pitons, which dangled forlornly on the handrail. A coating of verglas just beyond the Traverse boded ill for the rest of the route.

We reached the Swallow's Nest at 7 am. The Ice Hose presented no problem, but the normally easy rock slabs above wore a dangerous veneer of ice and Eric had a hard time leading up them. Time raced alarmingly and it was already 11 o'clock before we reached the Second Icefield. Traversing right to our previous cave on the Japanese Route, we spent the afternoon making ourselves at home and retrieving the food and equipment we had left there on our last visit. Everything in the cave was iced up. Even our medicinal whisky bottle was encased in a block of ice. Eric painstakingly chipped it out and revelries commenced.

26   *left*: Filming at the bottom of the Second Icefield shortly before I was hit by stonefall
27   *right*: The Hinterstoisser Traverse – a 100-foot steep slab of rock crossed by using a rope handrail

To harass me, knowing I had a phobia about bad meat, Eric suggested roguishly that the ham was 'off', and before we could stop him, Pete had grabbed it, held it to his completely defunct nose, sniffed, and pronounced it unfit. Then, to our great dismay, he chucked it overboard. Far below, in the wet cave by the Difficult Crack, two Scots lads were amazed to see the ham whizzing past, followed at intervals by odd gas cylinders and sodden marmalade.

We rose at dawn. Packing the camera and the rest of the gear took a couple of hours, but eventually we were back on the Second Icefield. Von Almen had mentioned a series of ledges on the rocks above the icefield and we hoped these would allow faster progress. It turned out that they too were so glazed with ice as to be unusable. The steep slope of the icefield ran straight into the rocks without any recess between. Traversing along the top was difficult and slow. Following Eric, I rapidly expanded my knowledge of ice technique. Then I belayed and Pete climbed up to me. I asked him to keep climbing until he almost banged his nose on the lens of the camera. Despite his lack of experience, he was wonderfully at ease as he tiptoed about nonchalantly on his crampon points.

This pattern continued; twenty roped pitches of traversing and tensioning along the top of the icefield, filming as we climbed. It seemed to go on interminably.

By the time we got near the Flatiron, the sun was high and its warmth was loosening the stones above. They cascaded into the Spider, ricocheted out of the bottom and strafed our route. To continue would have been lunacy. We decided to carve ourselves a ledge and bivouac here. It took us four hours of hard work to make a small platform on which to pass the night. I had kept a small bottle of brandy in reserve for trying situations, and this seemed one. Our slow, difficult progress and the hours of chopping away at the ice had sapped morale. The brandy did a magnificent job on our empty stomachs, and we grew carefree and lightheaded.

After dark we radioed Bob Brigham and Tony Johnson, who were in the Scheidegg Bar. The background chatter and chink of glasses served to heighten the unreality of our position, a tiny pinpoint of humanity in that vast white space.

Beneath the starry skies, the hills stretched far into the night, their icy tops floating above the deep milky mist in the valleys. It was a memorable night – the total isolation, the precariousness of our perch, the vista of mountains like a dream before us, the snugness of the bivouac, the warmth

28   Pete Minks climbing diagonally towards my camera position

of the brandy inside us, and, inevitably, the companionship. These formed
the essence of what one climbs for. And the fact that we had fought so
hard to reach this spot was an integral part of the pleasure. It would be
impossible to gain the same satisfaction by taking the train up the Jungfrau
on a similar night; that would be too easy and, should you get bored with
the view, would allow you to pop back to a warm hotel in your fur-lined
boots. For us, the experience was continuous and inescapable. We didn't
like to think of the next day's efforts. For the moment, experiencing the
crystalline night was more than enough. The stars swung on their way and
we slept beneath diamond skies.

Our cramped ledge added to the packing difficulties next morning. Pete's
casual strolling about without crampons was unnerving. I fully expected
him to slither off and shoot down the icefield, but his confidence in his
balance was not misplaced.

It was three pitches to the Flatiron and we found it littered with ropes
and pitons left by the Japanese on their second ascent of the Harlin Route.
The chimney, normally considered quite hard and rated Grade V, we
found easy, but heavy ice on the usually simple section to the top of the
Flatiron made that unexpectedly difficult and time-consuming.

It took us over two hours to reach the infamous Death Bivouac. The
delay left us with a problem. Should we continue and risk a poor bivouac
in the Ramp, or stay where we were and be certain of a dry and
comfortable night? We settled on the latter.

While Eric prepared the camp, Cliff and Pete started to fix ropes across
the Third Icefield. I wanted to film them but the camera refused to
function. Water on the film had jammed it. The film stuck in the gate and
the precious zoom lens was opaque with moisture on the inside. I
struggled with it for an hour, running it till it stopped, putting it in the
sun, extending the lens to maximise the effects of the sun's rays and
gradually losing my temper. Future parties no doubt marvelled at the
sight of 600 feet of cine film hanging down the face, tied to the pitons of
Sedlmayer and Mehringer. But eventually I got the camera to work, once
again recording our actions for posterity.

The sun went down below the horizon, but our morale stayed high as a
result of this third good bivouac. We were determined to keep going on
to the top, whatever the weather.

Fast progress was made on the fixed ropes across the Third Icefield next
morning, and soon I was filming Pete in the Ramp. The verglas added

29   Eric Jones on the Third Icefield. Death Bivouac is just out of sight around the corner.

greatly to our difficulties. The Grade IV pitch at the top was heavily iced and looked formidable. Pete thought that the variation Grade VI pitch looked easier. He led it with a full rucksack, continually shouting that it was hard and that he was in danger of falling off. But somehow he didn't. The rest of us followed, using our jumar clamps to climb up the rope. The pitch, we felt, was as hard as some of the *Extremely Severe* climbs in Wales, which would never be climbed in heavy boots and a rucksack. Pete's climb had been no mean effort.

As I arrived at the stance, I saw Pete about fifty feet above, tackling an ice bulge that dripped with gigantic icicles. He was laybacking up an icicle with the front points of one crampon barely gripping the ice wall level with his shoulder. We watched spellbound as he levered and scratched his way upwards. Reaching the top, he flung his axe over the bulge into the smooth ice of its dome. As he started to pull up on it, however, the axe head began to ease out of the ice. In desperation he smashed in his short axe too and slowly pulled up on that until the bulge was level with his stomach. From this position, cutting a step in the steep, hard ice above was a Herculean task, but he managed it. After watching this display, the rest of us came up on tight ropes. Even that proved difficult for it is almost impossible to secure a grip with crampons on very steep or overhanging ice while there is tension on the rope from above.

I was worn out by these exertions and felt disconsolate as I climbed slowly up the Brittle Ledges. This was the point of no return: no one had ever retreated from here in poor conditions. And conditions were definitely deteriorating now. Clouds had gathered and rain started to fall. The distant thunder approached rapidly. We huddled on the Brittle Ledges, making the most of their minimal shelter and worrying about our position. I slumped into a doze, exhausted, as the thunder crashed around us.

Suddenly, the other three leapt into the air, jerking convulsively. I could not understand what had happened. Then, I too was jarred into complete wakefulness as lightning struck again. My ice axe flew one way and I fell the other, against the ropes. We shivered, waiting for the next discharge to come stabbing at us out of nowhere and wondering if we could avoid it. Even Cliff was shaken. As he delivered a technical monologue on the arc gap we were in, we suddenly realised that it was our crampons that were causing the trouble. Never have I seen climbers discard their crampons, karabiners, pitons, hammers and axes so quickly. We threw all our ironware to the end of the ledge.

30 Crossing the Traverse of the Gods on the fifth day, with Grindelwald in the distance 8,000 feet
    below

The rocks overhung us, affording at least some shelter from the teeming rain. We decided to bivouac where we were on these narrow ledges. There was barely room to sit, and a drop below approaching 4,500 feet to the screes. If we could stay dry, our potential survival time increased to about four or five days. Somehow I had to keep the camera dry as well. It was an uncomfortable night. I cushioned my feet on a huge polythene bag full of snow which Eric had collected so that there would be no need to move in order to make a brew the next morning. We had so much sugar with us that I used two pounds of it in that tea to give us energy. It was surprisingly drinkable and nobody complained.

The climb up to the Traverse of the Gods on the fifth day again was difficult, and the Traverse itself – practically a walk in good conditions – turned out to be as hard as the Second Icefield. The climbing and filming were time-consuming and, despite our early start, the sun was striking the top of the mountain by the time we reached the Spider, one of the most dangerous places on the route. Stones fell from time to time and we grew apprehensive. Pete climbed up the ice slope above us, cutting steps and showering us with ice chippings. The higher he went, the harder they fell. In our tense, anxious state we were irritable and he soon came in for some heavy criticism. It was a ridiculous situation: four outraged people yelling furiously at each other in the middle of nowhere.

The others followed Pete into the Exit Cracks and I was left alone in the line of fire. Idly glancing up, I was horrified to see a huge rock, hundreds of feet above, toppling over and coming straight down towards me. As it bounced off the cliff, it shattered and burst into fragments, all heading for me. The time-honoured phrases flashed through my mind – 'This is it. I'm going to die!' As the bits clattered around me I made futile attempts to dodge them. Sharp stabs of pain accompanied the smaller hits. Then came a heavy blow which knocked me off my feet and left me stunned, hanging from one ice peg.

'Leo's been shot!' yelled Cliff, but I didn't appreciate the witticism.

As if to increase my misery, Pete began chopping again and more ice fragments cascaded down on me. My shrieked complaints were in vain. By the time I reached Eric I was exhausted. I had been bruised by big rocks, jabbed by small ones and showered in ice chips. I was thoroughly fed up and depressed, and had lost all desire to film the Eiger. I struggled on mindlessly.

Lack of protection added to our climbing difficulties. Pete forced himself up the Exit Cracks to the Corti Bivouac, a tiny pedestal leaning

31   Looking down the White Spider as Eric moved up towards me

32   *opposite:* Cliff tip-toeing on front points up the steep ice gully of the Exit Cracks
33   *above:* Our last night on the North Face, at the famous Corti Bivouac, a small ledge offering scarcely enough room for one

against the wall, as if glued to it. The others joined him, leaving me below, swathed in ropes, with all the sacks. My misery returned, and with it, paranoia. Poised on front points in the darkness, I hated the whole situation, and, not least, the others who had so skilfully dropped me in it. They hauled the other sacks up, but of course mine couldn't be hauled as the camera, tucked into the lid, would have been damaged. I was too exhausted to climb. They just had to haul me up too, dumping me and my sack unceremoniously in one corner of the tiny ledge.

Everything was chaotic. Sacks, ropes, gear and climbers, all piled in a jumbled heap. As we slowly gained control over the confusion, Cliff found a bit of black material sticking out of the snow, and, investigating, chipped away carefully. It turned out to be a 'corpse bag', abandoned by a rescue party, a grisly reminder of the Eiger's notoriety. When he threw it over the edge, it flapped down into the gloom like a great black bird of evil omen. I started thinking about Corti, after whom the place was named. Leaving his stricken companion below, he had climbed on alone, trying to get out, but on this little ledge, where we hung from our belays, he had stopped, unable to go further. I wondered what thoughts had gone through his mind as he sat there for three days, hungry, exhausted, alone, and slowly dying before Hellepart's merciful intervention.

The acoustics up here were uncanny. Eric dropped a saucepan and we could hear its tortuous passage down the Exit Cracks, the Spider, and the rest of the face. All sounds, however small, were caught and magnified in the great bowl of the upper wall – even the tinkle of a cowbell, drifting up from the placid meadows thousands of feet below. It was like being in the centre of a giant ear.

Very little food was left, and our second brew amounted only to a couple of mouthfuls each. We fell quiet, immersed in our solitary thoughts. Thirstily I dreamed of beer, millions of gallons of it – or even lemonade, or a tap, with me lying open-mouthed beneath it for eternity. The thought of food, too, real food, tormented me. Steak and chips, roast beef ... What on earth were we doing here? Down below there were food, drink, beds, comfort, good company – everything that makes life worth living. But for five days we had gone out of our way systematically to torture ourselves with exhaustion, danger, hunger, cold, thirst and a hundred other discomforts to get to this ridiculous place where we had nothing. What for? It was stupid. My tired brain could not reason it out.

I slumped forward. Immediately Eric fell back into my precious space, leaving me doubled up. I pushed and complained but he pretended to be asleep. I was furious. Trivial things assume enormous importance at times like this. Each of us became obsessed with the idea that the others were more comfortable than himself. However, I knew that Eric was a restless sleeper and, sure enough, after an hour he moved and I got my space back. We were miserably cramped, but at least we were warm. As well as all our ordinary gear, we were wearing all the stuff we had kept for emergencies. It no longer mattered – at least, so long as we didn't allow ourselves to relax. We were so near the top that there was a danger we might grow careless on those final verglassed cracks.

Next day, we pressed on. In the early afternoon we came out on to the final snow slopes and worked up towards the summit. The sun shone obliquely across the slope, picking out the detail. All around, green, menacing clouds heralded the storm promised days before. Suddenly, incredibly, the ordeal was over. All over, that is, bar the filming. We had reached the summit and Eric had been filmed taking the final steps, triumphantly waving his axes. But we still needed a close-up summit shot. And the film had run out ...

Anyone can load a cine camera standing out of the wind on flat, solid ground in reasonable temperatures. Here there was no flat ground; we

34　*above:* Pete and Cliff on the summit in late-afternoon light
35　*overleaf:* The footprints of Eric leading to the Eiger's summit, where he waves in triumph

were on a 60° ice slope, the temperature was freezing and the wind was so strong that I couldn't stand properly. My tired fingers dropped the first reel, and the second blew away. Swirling spindrift filled the eye-piece. Both wind and camera seemed to have minds of their own. Eric shielded me, and the third reel mercifully caught in the sprockets.

I supposed, fancifully, that a yeti would be better equipped than we were. But then a yeti would have more sense than to put himself in our position ... and anyway, yetis can't make films ... which of course was why we were here ... I was assuming it was a punishment for some evil deed ...

In the *Daily Mirror* of 9 December 1970, the day following the screening of my film, William Keenan acclaimed it as 'one of the most remarkable documentaries ever networked on ITV, exhilarating, fresh, inspiring, and reaching heights as magnificent as the Eiger itself.' He continued, 'It was, for me, and I'm sure for millions of viewers, the most dramatic mountaineering documentary ever made.'

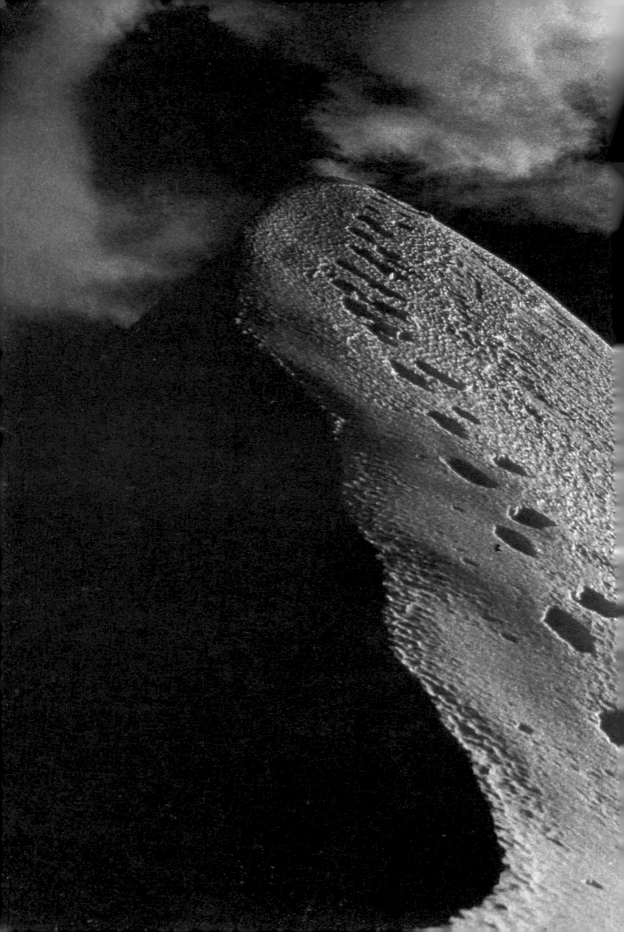

3
CERRO TORRE

'A solution awaiting a problem'

G. K. CHESTERTON ONCE SAID that it was one thing to be amazed by a gorgon or a griffin – creatures which do not exist – but quite another, and a much higher thing, to be amazed at a rhinoceros or a giraffe, creatures which *do* exist, but look as if they should not. It is much the same when you see Cerro Torre for the first time. Your eyes confirm its existence, yet reason all the while urges that it is most improbable, this slender finger of granite taunting the sky.

After our success on the Eiger, it seemed a natural progression to look further afield for even more spectacular adventures. You can't get much further afield than Patagonia and, unlike Nepal, an expedition there requires no Sherpas, no hassle with porters, no expedition doctor and no fee to be paid before even setting foot on your chosen mountain. Cerro Torre, in faraway Patagonia, then, seemed an ideal location for my next climbing film.

Chris Brasher of the BBC had phoned the day after our Eiger film was screened to say that I ought not to be making climbing films for Independent Television! What could I do for the BBC? We arranged a meeting, but before it took place, I went on a short skiing holiday to Austria with Bob Brigham and returned with a leg broken in twelve

36   *above:* The Headwall of Cerro Torre, shortly after a storm. This is the top section opposite.
37   *opposite:* The classical view of Cerro Torre: (right-hand skyline) the route described by Maestri in 1959 leading up the overhanging mushrooms of ice to the summit, (bottom right) the triangular snowpatch from where Toni Egger was swept away and killed, and (left-hand skyline) the South-west Ridge, which attracted two strong British expeditions as well as Maestri and his infamous compressor

places. As an intrepid mountaineer and cameraman, I painted a sorry picture hobbling on crutches along the Corridors of Power in the BBC. Still, by the time Chris poured the second bottle of wine, he was ready to overlook my disability, and we got down to details. I had persuaded him that Cerro Torre would make a fine 'World About Us' feature, and once the Irish Coffee arrived, we had persuaded ourselves that Cerro Torre was in reality little more than the Old Man of Hoy with ice on it. It should give us no problems!

We enlarged our original Eiger team with the addition of Swiss climber Hans Peter Trachsel and Yorkshireman Gordon Hibberd. Gordon had soloed the Lauper Route on the Eiger, and Hans had climbed the Eiger's notorious North Face no less than three times – once by the North-east Pillar, once by the classic 1938 route, which we had filmed, and also by the Japanese direct route.

Four weeks later, our Eiger quartet of Pete, Cliff, Eric and myself arrived in Buenos Aires and checked into a sleazy hotel. If ever there was a case of Innocents Abroad, it was us. I had no clear idea where Cerro Torre was and none of us could speak a word of Spanish. Only Gordon had been to these shores before, having climbed The Fortress in the Paine Group with Ian Clough, but he and Hans had set off a few days earlier as an advance party and were now 1,500 miles further south. There, some days later, in the little shanty town of Río Gallegos, we all met up before setting out on the 200-mile drive to the National Park of FitzRoy, where our mysterious mountain was to be found. With the help of local gauchos, we moved all the equipment to our base camp within a week, settled in and were ready to start our attack on the mountain.

For over 5,000 miles the Andean Cordillera stretches as an elongated spine down the South American continent to the isolated fjords and lakes of the Magellan Straits, then as a final thrust, rises out of the sea again in Tierra del Fuego and bristles on towards Cape Horn. The Paine and the FitzRoy massifs are the main mountain blocks, each a collection of steep granite spires about 100 miles apart; they are separated by a straight chain of rocky peaks and bounded to the west by the Patagonian Ice Cap. The FitzRoy massif is the higher and more impressive of the two, yet even this rises to only just above 11,000 feet. Nevertheless, these jagged peaks offer some of the hardest climbing in the world. The rock is good, stripped of any weakness by the harsh weather, and tremendously steep, giving a sense of

38   *opposite:* The Headwall of Cerro Torre in high wind
39   *overleaf:* Mount FitzRoy in evening light, where the milky shaded sky forecasts stormy
      weather

exposure akin to the great walls of the Dolomites. But here the similarity ends, for the sun rarely has that comfortable measure of Italian warmth and the wind, when it blows, hurls itself across the wastes of ice, gathering into itself a deep, deep cold. It tears at the rocky spires, leaving a quick crust of sheet ice across the holds and turning fixed ropes into useless columns of ice, while tracing its path along the ridges with a white scar of frost. The treacherous weather has guarded these mountains from attaining the degree of popularity enjoyed by the Himalayas and other equally remote ranges. *The Land of Tempest* is the title Eric Shipton gave to his book describing the exploratory journeys he had made in Patagonia, and it is a title that sums up the region exactly. If a climber is lucky, he may have two or three spells of good weather during an expedition. On the other hand, and equally likely, he may have none. The changes occur without warning. The Patagonian weather gods do not work subtly, they do not gradually shade a blue sky with grey, or gently build up the wind so that the mountaineer, detecting its tell-tale whisperings across the rock, or the warning dullness in the sky, can retreat. Rather, they tip ice out of an empty sky and dispatch their winds in sudden stampeding herds.

Cerro FitzRoy – named after the captain of the *Beagle*, which, with Charles Darwin aboard, performed much of the early exploration of the Magellan channels and the rivers of Patagonia – was the first of the central Patagonian peaks to attract explorers and mountaineers. It usually wears a plume of mist on its summit, which deceived the early Indians into believing it to be a volcano. They called it *Chalten*, which remains its official name in Chile. Having repelled a series of attempts by mountaineers from Italy and Austria over a fifteen-year span, FitzRoy was eventually climbed in 1952 by a French expedition, led by Lionel Terray, that redoubtable and self-styled Conquistador of the Useless. He wrote afterwards that of all his climbs, this was the one on which he most nearly approached his physical and mental limits. While it might, technically speaking, have been slightly less extreme than some of the granite climbs being accomplished in the Alps at that time, nevertheless a great ascent is more than the sum of its several pitches. The remoteness of FitzRoy from any possibility of help, its almost incessant bad weather, the black ice with which it is plastered and, above all, its terrible winds, all render it more complex, hazardous and exhausting than anything to be found in the Alps.

With reason, the ascent of FitzRoy attracted considerable attention in mountaineering circles and a book of the expedition was brought out by M. A. Azema, in which he described the nearby 'nightmare aiguilles' of Cerro Torre:

From a bubbling devil's cauldron, where clouds heavy as pitch boiled up from the depths and eddies of snow chased each other in the gale, there emerged at intervals the summits of the Cerro Torre and its satellites. Like immovable reefs in a raging sea, the black slabs reared up towards the sky to be smothered by the stupendous ice caps, sparkling with fresh snow, which overhung on all sides – glittering lighthouses whose foundations were submerged in foam.

Other climbers were quick to rise to such a lure. Several European expeditions attempted Cerro Torre, including one led by Bruno Detassis, a well-known Dolomite guide. He pronounced the Torre 'impossible' and forbade his team to attempt it! Walter Bonatti and Carlo Mauri were the star climbers in a private Italian expedition which was concurrently attempting the mountain from its opposite, western, side. After a forty-mile trek-in, they were encouraged by relatively easy ground leading to a col on the main ridge. Here they encountered for the first time the ice-bound overhanging walls which made them realise how the dangers and difficulties of Cerro Torre had been grossly underestimated. The climbers turned back after deciding to call their highest point the Col of Hope.

Clearly they intended to return for another bid as soon as possible, but were beaten to it by another Italian, Cesare Maestri. In 1959 he claimed the first ascent of Cerro Torre. He had reached the summit, he said, following a route on the East Face with an Austrian climber, Toni Egger, who was subsequently killed by an avalanche on the way down. Maestri himself was found distraught and half-buried in snow at the foot of the peak, alone, some days later.

It was an incredible tale and Lionel Terray, one of those to have scaled FitzRoy, declared that it was the greatest mountaineering feat of all time. Maestri returned to a hero's welcome, the whole town of Trento turning out to greet him and his companions.

For the next ten years Cerro Torre was left alone, but, as harder and harder walls were climbed, Maestri's declared route on Cerro Torre began to look even more impossible and ahead of its time. It was inconceivable that he should have lied about getting to the summit, yet doubts were beginning to be whispered.

By the time we arrived at the foot of Cerro Torre in 1971, British climbers had already failed in one attempt on the South-east Ridge of the mountain. A Lecco team with Carlo Mauri and Casimiro Ferrari had climbed to within 630 feet of the summit via the West Face, and Maestri himself had twice been back to Cerro Torre to climb the South-east Ridge.

There were of course no guidebooks to Cerro Torre and our information was limited to a magazine article by Maestri on his first ascent, and an account of the 1968 British team's attempt on the South-east Ridge. This had been a strong party, which had chosen this route because it appeared to be the easiest ridge of the mountain, avoiding the hazard of falling ice that had made Maestri's route so appalling. Even so, despite their combined expertise and the best equipment available, the Britons were beaten back by bad weather and difficult rock and ice pitches. We had decided to go for the same South-east Ridge, hoping to pick up the gauntlet where they had dropped it. In the meantime we had heard rumours that Maestri had returned and finished the line with the aid of some strange device, but exact details were very sketchy.

From the foot of the mountain we could see the line of Maestri's first ascent route and gaped at it in wonder. It made the North Face of the Eiger look like a Sunday afternoon stroll and we were glad to be trying the South-east Ridge instead.

Having organised our advanced base on the glacier at the foot of the mountain, we climbed 2,000 feet to the Col of Patience, as Pete Crew had so aptly named it, where we dug ourselves a snow cave to house all six of us – modestly. From here our attentions were directed upwards to the East Arête. Naturally, we expected to come across some relics of previous traffic, but in no way were we prepared for the extent of the jetsam we discovered. At first there were just the odd bolts and a few pitons and lengths of frayed rope, but then, after 1,000 feet, we came to a platform where as many as fifteen 'bolts' had been splattered, seemingly at random, as if fired from a machine gun.

By 'bolts', I mean that holes had been driven into the granite to enable expansion bolts to be inserted, as opposed to the more usual piton placement in natural cracks and fissures. It can be argued that there is some artistry in placing pitons which rely on the rock's natural features, but bolts can be inserted anywhere to lead the climber up the steepest, barest rock. Cerro Torre is made of some of the hardest granite in the world, and to drill a hole into it would normally be a very tiring and time-consuming process. These carelessly broadcast bolts signified something entirely new. We had encountered dramatic evidence of Maestri's further assaults on Cerro Torre.

When questions first began to be asked about his original climb,

40   *above*: Looking out of our ice cave at FitzRoy from the Col on the South-east Arête of Cerro Torre
41   *below*: Inside the cramped ice cave I pour out a brew of hot tea that started life as part of the ceiling

Maestri had seemed reluctant to answer. Once doubts were being voiced openly, Maestri's typically self-confident assertion was that for all he knew, there might be *no one* else in the world capable of repeating Cerro Torre. Such bravado did little to gain him widespread sympathy. Eleven years after his first ascent – the year in fact we were filming on the Eiger – Maestri returned to Cerro Torre with a strong team and an even more persuasive weapon – a pneumatic drill. He was determined to climb the mountain again, dramatically and indisputably. If and when the climbing became too difficult, he would simply make a bolt ladder to the summit. Now we were seeing for ourselves the extent of his pneumatic drilling.

When we came to the first of Maestri's bolt ladders, we were not quite sure how to handle it. We had not travelled halfway round the world just to climb a prepared stairway. Yet here we were, confronted with an impassable sheet of ice; the only possible way to avoid it was to follow Maestri's bolt line. With misgivings, much argument and self-criticism, we took Maestri's route. No one was happy about it, no one could really justify it, and morale deteriorated faster than the weather. But where *do* you draw the line? To use one peg left by the British expedition, one bolt of Maestri's . . . six bolts of Maestri's . . . ten? A hundred? We could always have argued that we wanted to see the extent of the damage, but after two months of recurring bad weather and a distinct lack of enthusiasm for this despoiled route, we retreated, our tails between our legs. Our brilliant team, which had done so well in the Alps, had come unstuck. We brought home a fairly average 'World About Us' film, but had hoped for so much more.

Time passed. I went to Patagonia again to cross the Ice Cap, and yet again the following year to attempt Cerro Torre's satellite peak, Torre Egger. In 1974 the Italian climber Casimiro Ferrari organised an assault on Cerro Torre from the west. He drew his team from among members of the *Gruppo Ragni* (the Spiders), an élite climbing group from Lecco, and was successful in making an undisputed ascent. Two years later, while making an attempt on Torre Egger, an Anglo-American party discovered the grim remains of Toni Egger. Maestri had always maintained that Egger carried the camera with proof of their ascent on film, but sadly, no camera was found with the body. So the mystery of the Maestri-Egger climb remained.

Meanwhile, as events marched on, the film I had taken on Cerro Torre, as well as some material I had shot earlier of an interview with Cesare Maestri, was rapidly falling into the category 'historical'. It occurred to me to make a documentary film tracing the whole fascinating story of this mysterious mountain at the bottom of the world, and the equally mysterious man, Cesare Maestri, who claimed twice to have climbed it.

I began to collect together all the intrinsic evidence I could find. Articles and chapters written by Maestri and others were, for the first time, translated into English, and a flurry of letters travelled backwards and forwards to Italy. I was determined to give Maestri as much say in my film as those who discredited his claim of a first ascent.

In 1959 when he had made his climb, Cesare Maestri was twenty-nine. He was a climber with a phenomenal reputation in his native Italy, having got up vertical limestone faces by improbable routes throughout the 1950s, earning himself the nickname 'Spider of the Dolomites'. Eager to push himself to the limit, mentally and physically, he would undertake the hardest climbs alone and then climb back down, rather than roping off or finding an alternative, easier way down.

His friend Cesarino Fava had suggested they might try the mountain back in 1953, but it was several years before they eventually laid hands upon it. Maestri had been a member of Bruno Detassis's abortive 1958 expedition, then in 1959 he returned with among others Fava and Toni Egger, the latter an Austrian climber with a formidable reputation on ice. They attacked the East Face which rises about 5,000 feet above the glacier. At first, Toni Egger was out of action with a boil on his foot, and Maestri climbed with Fava. Fava himself had lost some toes through frostbite on an earlier expedition and was, by his own admission, not in the same class as Maestri. Nevertheless, progress was good. After eleven days they had equipped three camps leading to the foot of the face and begun some serious climbing. The lower section turned out to be cut by a groove 1,200 feet high, leading to a small snowfield. The climbing was of a high standard and the best equipment was used to assail the steep rocks.

Maestri later described to me in a letter the method he used, one he and Egger had previously tried many times in hazardous conditions, with excellent results. 'This technique consists of exploiting the low mounds of ice or the stretches of packed snow, climbing with crampons and ice axes, and then implanting regular threaded bolts or long specially-made devices into the fissures. (These were obtained from water-pipes, cut into salami-like pieces for the purpose.) It also involved inserting serrated wedges of aluminium between the rocks and ice . . .' He added, 'Taking part in the first Trento Expedition to the Torre, led by Bruno Detassis, I realised then that the usual techniques would be of very little value when attempting a mountain constantly subjected to the rigours of alternate freezing and thawing.'

With each day's progress, ropes were fixed so that an easy descent could be made to the ice cave at the foot of the face for the night. The next day the ropes would be reascended to the highest point and climbing begun again.

Fava later described some of the climbing above Camp III:

> Cesare goes back up to the last piton, then away above the fissure with his unmistakable style and elegance. From the way he climbs it looks relatively easy; he goes up about 150 metres, then tells me to follow him. I cling to the 12 mm hemp rope which will remain fixed to the wall, do a pendulum swing to get myself over to a point beneath the vertical, and start. From the way *I* climb, belayed to Cesare, I am made fully aware of his extraordinary ability and class and can fully appreciate why he is called the Spider.

By the end of January, Egger had completely recovered and the route was equipped as far as the icefield. On 27 January Maestri, Egger and Fava were all back in Camp III and an interesting candlelit discussion took place, which turned out to have a critical bearing on the outcome of the expedition. Fava recalled later:

> Cesare was convinced that we should also fix ropes on the Second Dihedron which leads to the Col and then make a good bivouac there. Toni, on the other hand, thought the best technique would be that already used on Jirishanca – in other words, to go up with everything we needed and be independent for five or six days. He said it would be quicker and less tiring. Cesare accepted his argument, but pointed out, rightly, that it would be impossible to carry everything they needed. At this point it was obvious to me that my support would be of great help, but I also realised that he didn't want me to feel obliged. 'Boys,' I said, 'I am several years your senior. As for my personal safety, the responsibility is mine, so let *me* decide that for myself. If you need my help, then as far as I can, I'll go with you.'

So an alpine-style ascent was decided upon. They would take enough food for several days, a sleeping bag and as many ropes, pitons and so on as they could carry, then go like hell for the summit. It was a staggeringly bold plan of Egger's, especially in those days, but Maestri and Fava both endorsed it.

42   *above left:* Cesare Maestri
43   *above right:* Toni Egger
44   *below:* Filming halfway up the South-east Ridge of Cerro Torre with my faithful Canon Scoopic; the Mocho can be seen a few thousand feet below and the lake near our base camp some miles away
45   *overleaf:* Cerro Torre by moonlight. The white streak is Venus.

The next day the three of them climbed to the Col of Conquest – so named by Maestri, seemingly in defiance of his compatriots Bonatti and Mauri, who had christened the opposing South-west Col, Col of Hope. Maestri maintained that there was no place for hope in mountains, only the will to conquer. Hope, he said, is the weapon of the poor.

It was afternoon when they reached the Col. Above them rose the final 2,500 feet of the Torre. Fava, having helped them carry up the equipment required for the frozen North Wall, prepared for a solo descent. The other two would continue upwards the next morning if the weather held good. Fava lowered himself down the fixed ropes, regaining the glacier as the last rays of January sun faded from the topmost mountain pinnacles. He settled in to wait for his comrades.

During the next two days Maestri and Egger battled their way up the steep rock of the North Ridge and through the overhanging summit ice mushrooms without fixed ropes. Maestri, without very much detail, has told of the climb and how as they began their descent from the top, the weather grew dangerously warm. Snow started to melt and avalanche down all sides of the mountain and there was a very high wind. The climbers were running short of food after another bivouac, and the next day, 300 feet above the relative safety of their fixed ropes, just as they were preparing to spend a further night out on the steep snow-patch below the level of the Col, disaster struck.

Out of the mist a huge avalanche suddenly appeared, shrieking down the East Face like an express train. It was upon the climbers like a flash of lightning. Maestri, clinging to the ropes at the belay point, managed to hang on; Egger, sixty feet lower down the rope, was overwhelmed and swept away. The rucksacks of both men were also taken.

Shocked and bewildered by the sudden death of Egger, Maestri waited sleeplessly till morning, then made his way down the fixed ropes. He slipped on some ice near the foot of the wall and slithered and tumbled down the mountain, beyond the pile of avalanche debris, over the crevasse at the bottom, and came to rest on a small platform on the glacier. From that moment on he can recall nothing of what happened until he was rescued.

Fava, meanwhile, after waiting anxiously for five days and six nights at Camp III, reluctantly decided the two men were not coming back, and, on the morning of 3 February, set off slowly down towards Camp II, taking advantage of the intermittent bright intervals. During one of these, he glanced back towards the Torre and noticed a strange dark speck on the glacier. He put it down to a crevasse shadow. A few minutes later, when he looked back again and found it still there, he decided to trudge back and investigate, urged, he said, more by conscience than hope. As he drew nearer he had the distinct impression that the dark spot was moving and gradually it took on a vaguely human shape. Fava quickened his pace. Half-buried in the snow above the lip of a crevasse, it now definitely appeared to be a man. But which of the two was it?

As he approached, Fava could see it was Maestri. It was his anorak that had saved him. The snow had been unable to cling to its smooth surface and this had been what Fava spotted from the distance. Only three words escaped through Maestri's teeth and ice-encrusted beard: 'Toni, Toni, Toni . . .' Fava led him down to safety.

The ascent of Cerro Torre was generally heralded to be a breakthrough in Alpine climbing. Maestri had taken an appalling risk and alone had survived after immense suffering and endurance. His fellow townsfolk of Trento awarded him a special gold medal.

It was Carlo Mauri, Maestri believes, who started speculation about the veracity of the climb with an article in *Il Corriere*. In it, Mauri stopped short of actually saying that Maestri had *not* made it to the summit. Indeed, Maestri maintains that if he *had*, he would have admired him more. 'I would have sued him, but I would have respected him.' Instead, Mauri just talked about the mountain as if it had never been climbed, completely ignoring Maestri's ascent. He even referred to the mountain as impossible. As the controversy snowballed, Maestri's first reaction was to return to Cerro Torre and climb it again.

> Let me put it this way – suppose you worked in a bank and, just before you were to retire, you heard a rumour that you had walked off with £10,000 of the bank's money, what would you do? Would you go to court and try to prove your innocence, or, if there was some way in which you could clear your name by one theatrical gesture, would you not choose that? Even if it involved a certain amount of danger to yourself, wouldn't you take the latter course?

Maestri's return to Cerro Torre in 1971 was his theatrical gesture. Although the South-east Ridge had already beaten three other expeditions, it seemed the safest and easiest of the Torre's three ridges and Maestri settled for that. Its appearance was deceptive. It was very narrow with few alternative lines, cloaked with snow and ice and fully exposed to the raging Antarctic winds. The 1968 British expedition had failed above the Col and below the overhanging ice cornices that are such a major obstacle high on the mountain. No one had ever set foot on the 700-foot headwall, nor the forbidding snow mushrooms just below the summit.

For Maestri, however, there could be no question of failure. He helicoptered in a strong team with a wooden hut for base camp as protection against the formidable weather. Instead of making his attempt in the traditional summer season, he was to climb right in the middle of winter. Soon the hut was well buried with snow, making a snug refuge for the team. Outside the conditions were fierce, the temperature often −13°F, the winds never less than 30 mph, often gusting to almost 100.

Of the fifty-four consecutive days they worked on the wall, they were forced to spend twenty-eight nights bivouacking in hammocks. One other factor contributed to their slow progress: the weight of gear they were winching up the face. They were employing a weapon never before used by man against mountain. Up these precipitous heights, they carried 3 cwt of petrol, oil, winches, ropes and a motor compressor – to drive a pneumatic drill. But *why* the compressor and drill? Maestri replied: 'I took it because I calculated I might have to hammer in up to 1,000 bolts. Of course this would have been an endless process by normal means.' He went on to explain that the decision had not presented him with any philosophical problems:

> I have spent most of my life trying to push forward the limits of climbing and climbing techniques in general. I did this with solo climbing – I have soloed Grade 6 routes in both ascent and descent. When all the other expeditions started failing on the South-east Ridge of Cerro Torre, despite the fact that they were all comprised of good climbers, it seemed to me that the route must be impossible by normal means, so I decided bolting would be necessary.

As it turned out, the heavy gear proved more of a burden than a blessing. The hauling took three hours every time they wanted to use the drill. More than 300 bolts were placed, mainly around stances, but this was far fewer than Maestri had envisaged and he felt afterwards that a hand–drill would have served him better. In the face of the cries of 'Desecration!' and 'Rape!' he remained unrepentant, likening the drill to a plastic pole in pole-vaulting. 'When this came in,' he said, 'the world record was immediately broken, yet the skill of the athlete was in no way diminished. In the same way, the compressor is just an improvement on existing techniques and it does not detract in any way from the climber's ability.'

46   *above*: An ice storm striking Cerro Torre, Torre Egger and (right) Torre Stanhardt, making any movement, either up or down, impossible

47   *below*: At dawn the sun just lights up the top section of Cerro Torre and the mushroom on top of Torre Egger

Despite all the bolting up 1,200 feet of virgin rock, despite two visits to finish the job, Maestri's team didn't quite make it to the very top of Cerro Torre. They declined to climb the 150-foot-high summit mushroom. 'It's just a lump of ice,' Maestri rationalised, 'not really part of the mountain. It'll blow away one of these days.'

Instead of clearing his name, Maestri had rushed headlong into yet another and noisier controversy. 'How could Maestri,' demanded *Mountain* magazine, 'a man who claimed to have ascended one of the world's hardest mountains in perhaps the boldest and finest climb of all time, think of returning to make a second ascent by means of such despicable tactics, thus befouling and polluting the whole aura surrounding the peak?'

His defence was simple. To his critics he merely said, 'I fought against the Nazis in the war as a partisan, and this has given me certain views on life in general and on my climbing in particular. I consider that any form of imposition on the individual comes under the heading of Fascism ... I do not believe that *any*body has the right to lay down the law about what is, and what is not, a genuine form of climbing.'

There had been eleven expeditions to Cerro Torre and so far only Cesare Maestri claimed to have been to the summit. In 1974 when Casimiro Ferrari took up the challenge with his team from Lecco there were to be no pneumatic drills, only normal climbing equipment – although they did allow themselves the indulgence of having a priest flown in to pray for success!

Ferrari decided on the West Face, which is the shortest on the mountain, although it involves a very much longer approach march. Within three days of arrival, they had established a camp within 1,500 feet of the summit. Then there followed three weeks during which they had to sit out a fearful storm. All the time a handful of climbers stayed in their top camp, ready to launch an attempt as soon as conditions improved. When they did, it was for too short a time to get fresh supplies up to the men, and another prolonged wait ensued.

Finally, on the thirteenth day, the weather improved and Ferrari with three companions made a desperate and successful bid for the summit. The overhanging snow mushroom presented serious difficulties, but the four finally traversed three long pitches around it and were able to force a way through to the top. Now Cerro Torre had been indisputably climbed. The four men built a snowman on top in tribute to their Lecco club, took some hasty summit pictures, then started the long descent. (Ironically, their pictures proved little more than Maestri's lost ones since the summit was reached in a white-out.)

If these four men had succeeded in such continuously bad weather, might not then Maestri and Egger – who was known for his daring speed and skill – also have done it, if they had enjoyed better snow conditions? The proof lay, as it still does, in Egger's camera buried deep in the huge glacier at the foot of the tower.

The American climber Jim Donini, who was in the area with Mick Coffey, Ben Campbell-Kelly and Brian Wyvill in 1975, trying to make an alpine ascent of Cerro Standhardt, the third sister in the Torre group, was coming down the steep glacier to where it levelled off at the bottom of the Cirque, when some things were discovered on the ice.

'Mick Coffey called us over,' Donini related for my film, 'and we found what were the remains of Toni Egger. Now Toni was killed fifteen years earlier and in that time, his body had come about a mile and a half down the glacier and then melted out. What we found were just a boot here, a boot there. We found the rope he had been abseiling on when the ice avalanche hit him. We found his ice axe, we found various things. We didn't find the camera ... but then again, there were a lot of things we didn't find. There can be no doubt that it was Toni's body because of its position and the equipment, the boots made in Kitzbühel and everything else. Along with that, he is the only person to have been killed in that area. The camera, if it does still exist at all, may be under a few metres of ice. We felt that this was a good resting place for a climber, so we left his body there. We did take a karabiner which had been close by and the next year, when we climbed Torre Egger, the peak adjacent to Cerro Torre and named after Toni, we left the karabiner on the summit. It was in fact the only thing we did leave on the summit.'

On that Torre Egger climb in 1976, Donini made further discoveries which once more opened up the Maestri controversy. The route his team took was by way of the Col of Conquest, following the line of Maestri and Egger. Initially, Donini recalls, he had been one of the few people to believe Maestri's story. Maestri had an enviable record and Donini took him at his word: 'When somebody like Cesare Maestri says he's climbed the most difficult mountain in the world, you believe him.' For Donini, climbing up to the Col of Conquest turned out to be incredibly difficult. In my film interview he said:

I expected something more in line with alpine climbing, more of a mixed type of ground – a hard pitch, an easier pitch, a little bit of snow, a little bit of rock. It turned out in fact to be very, very continuous – a lot of it of the nature of Yosemite big wall climbing. A number of hanging belays, a number of difficult nailing pitches, artificial aids ... it was a climb on a big, scary mountain. Ice climbing, too, so that just doing the first 3,000 feet to the Col of Conquest was for me more difficult than any of the routes I had done on El Capitan. It was very, very interesting.

I remember in the first seven or eight hundred feet finding all sorts of remains of Maestri's route – little shards of rope hanging from wafer pitons and wooden wedges. I hadn't seen wooden wedges before. In Yosemite we had all the modern gear. I know the Dolomites are studded with wooden wedges – so, for me, it was very interesting to find a wooden wedge, to find two, to find ten in a row. They left a lot of equipment behind: pitons, wedges, ropes – you name it, it was there. So we were following history as we climbed the first thousand feet. It helped us find the correct way. Essentially they had done the route finding for us.

We got very close to a large, very prominent terrain feature on Cerro Torre, the triangular snowfield that is about a thousand feet up, and, with high cirrus moving in and the possibility of a storm coming in the next day, we thought we could push a few pitches through and get up to the snowfield that day. I remember belaying John Bragg from a hanging position on a vertical granite wall, while he did a difficult traverse and then climbed up a beautiful runnel of ice. After that there was another easier ice pitch, and then it was my lead and I moved back left and found a 100-foot aid pitch bristling with gear left behind by Maestri and Egger. For a hundred feet, a piton was fixed about every three and a half or four feet. And through every piton there was a karabiner – which was very, very puzzling . . . I couldn't figure it out. Through the karabiners went a rope, and the rope was clove-hitched or tied to about every other karabiner. This pitch ended on a very small, sloping ledge about fifty feet below the snowfield, and on this ledge we found a pack with old wooden wedges and pitons and three or four ropes next to the pack. It was an obvious equipment dump.

So we had this fixed pitch and the equipment dump – and, above that, a fifty foot overhanging blank wall, and then the snowfield, and then, from there to the Col of Conquest itself, 2,000 feet of what we found to be very sustained and very difficult climbing. But we found nothing else: no pitons, no shards of rope, no wooden wedges . . . no bootprints in the snow. Nothing at all. There was no further evidence of previous passage from 1959.

48   From a high vantage point on the opposite side of the valley to Cerro Torre, the three granite fingers are seen against the backdrop of the Patagonian Ice Cap

It was easy to see the question marks forming in Donini's mind. He went on:

> Maybe, then, they went a different way. It is possible. From the snowfield there were two obvious lines, one up a very steep ice gully and the other on to beautiful crack systems to the right of the gully on a rock buttress. We were thinking about the ice gully. We got to it, but it was a rampaging avalanche-chute, incredibly dangerous. Just to cross it, to get over to the rock buttress, was a very scary proposition – but that's the way we had to go. So we crossed the ice gully and went up these beautiful crack systems for a thousand feet. Very difficult fun-climbing if it weren't for the fact that the ice mushrooms were 3,000 feet above you, just looming there, waiting to drop.
>
> After 1,500 feet of sustained climbing, we came to what we thought from below would be a problem. We didn't know exactly how to traverse into the Col. Maestri and Egger presumably had done it in '59 but from below it looked unreasonable. We couldn't see anything until we turned a corner and, lo and behold, hidden from below, was a nice ramp, that gave us comparatively easy access to the Col of Conquest. We found nothing there either – no rappel anchors, no fixed pitons left behind, nothing at all. If you found a piton you would know that they got to this point, without a shadow of doubt they got this far. The fact that we *didn't* find any pitons doesn't however conclusively mean they *didn't* get to this point. It's very suspicious, in my eyes it's very damning. But it's not conclusive.

The Americans' climb to the Col of Conquest took much longer than expected. Not counting the ups and downs of getting stormed off and retreating, the total climbing time to the Col was about six days. Was it possible that Maestri and Egger could have done it in much less? Maestri had said:

> Our progress was helped by exceptionally good conditions and we climbed by ordinary ice techniques. But remember, Cerro Torre is very close to the Antarctic; the condition of the ice is unique, it's unstable and very dangerous. Toni Egger was an exceptional ice climber and, thanks to his brilliant technique, we dealt with all the difficulties very quickly.

Donini finds it hard to believe that the Europeans could have climbed faster than they had themselves, even by using more artificial aid. So, who does Jim Donini feel made the first ascent of Cerro Torre? Was it Maestri in 1959, or was it Casimiro Ferrari in 1974? 'Given the spirit of mountaineering, one would like to give Maestri the benefit of the doubt, but after having repeated two to three thousand feet of Maestri's route, I personally have grave reservations.'

Few climbers who stand on the summit of a peak for the first time are ever asked to prove it. Their word is usually sufficient. And indeed, proof may often be difficult or impossible to produce. The summit may be reached in darkness or in cloud, deep snow may quickly bury anything left behind. No one queried whether Hermann Buhl reached the summit of Nanga Parbat in 1953, nor indeed that the Messner brothers stood on that same summit in 1970. It is usually a question of mutual trust between climbers. Yet, for some reason, in Maestri's case that trust would seem to have mutually broken down.

I wrote to Maestri when I was editing the film and told him of the queries raised by Jim Donini's account. He replied that he thought the cause of all this speculation was the fact that many climbers mistakenly believed that his ascent was made over rock, whereas it was – apart from the first 300 to 350 metres – in fact a very hazardous ascent on ice. And he described how, on returning to the South-east Ridge for his second attempt, using his patent threaded bolts system again, long stretches of gear had totally disappeared, leaving only exposed areas of very smooth and extremely difficult rock. And that was within a period of three months only. What then could happen in a decade and a half?

Yet, if Maestri did climb Cerro Torre in 1959, *why* did he go back to do it again by another route, and with such a flagrant disregard for climbing ethics? Jim Donini summed it up at the end of the film when he said, 'We'll never know, we'll never really know.' It is impossible to prove either way. If the elusive camera were to turn up, it would probably prove nothing; it is very unlikely the film would still be printable after coming down two glacier systems, through all those years of cold and heat and water.

People tend to be sceptical and often doubt extraordinary feats instinctively unless witnessed with their own eyes. Even then we sometimes wish the facts would go away. In the Mexico Olympics Bob Beamon in the long-jump event, despite the rarefied air, nearly jumped out of the pit. If millions of people had not witnessed Beamon's jump, or if the judges had not measured it with their tape measures, it would never have been believed, especially as Beamon himself has never been able to produce another jump remotely like it. Scepticism is further heightened when other likely performers fail to match the superhuman feat. This clearly is an ingredient in the Cerro Torre story.

Early in 1981 two British climbers, Phil Burke and Tom Proctor, succeeded in climbing the East Face of Cerro Torre to within the few final feet of the soggy and overhanging summit mushroom. In places they were retracing the route Maestri claimed to have taken. Like Donini, they found the lines of pegs, bolt clusters and remnants of fixed rope on the way up to the icefield. Then there were two rucksacks and ropes tied to a piton, and from that point on, nothing else that could positively be attributed to an earlier passage. The chimney Maestri said they climbed was, as Donini had also observed, an avalanche gutter accepting the bulk of the snow and ice shed from the summit. The icy gullies on the upper part of the North Face were exceptionally steep and difficult, and the spot where Maestri

49   Cerro Torre and FitzRoy against the setting sun

said Egger and he spent their last bivouac turned out to be in a suicidal position.

Once again, these facts do not represent hard evidence, one way or the other, and the two British climbers sensibly refrained from passing any judgment. The paradox still remains and doubtless speculation will continue. Perhaps, after all, that makes the better story. Many climbers – including myself – would *like* to believe that against all the odds, Maestri and Egger succeeded in making it to the top of Cerro Torre in 1959. Only one man perhaps knows the answer for certain – Maestri himself.

4
LAND OF MIST
AND FIRE:
EXPLORING THE
PATAGONIAN ICE
CAP

These vast piles of snow which never melt
and seem destined to last as long as the
world holds together present a noble and
sublime spectacle.
Charles Darwin, The Voyage of the
Beagle, *1823*

IN 1520, three centuries before Darwin's voyage in the *Beagle*, Magellan's ship reached the southernmost tip of South America. During the long hours at sea he had passed the time reading a book about Greek romantic chivalry, in which the hero had captured a monster called the Grand Patagon. The creature had the head of a dog, was gifted with human understanding and was amorous of women. When tormented, it roared like a bull. To Magellan's astonishment, when he made landfall, he was greeted by a naked giant, dancing and leaping and throwing sand on its head. When captured, the native let out a fearful bellow and so, legend has it, Magellan was prompted to utter, 'Ah! Patagon!' And so Patagonia, the land of the Patagon, gained its name. This remote region at the extreme tip of Latin America conceals one of the least-explored places on earth, the Patagonian Ice Cap, 9,000 square miles of crevassed ice.

The idea of mounting an expedition to the Patagonian Ice Cap came one day when Eric Jones and I were trapped in our tents by a storm on Cerro Torre. While the violent weather we were experiencing precluded upward progress, involving as it did very difficult climbing, it did not seem to us that it would necessarily prevent *horizontal* travel. We decided to return the following summer and put our theory to the test on the Ice Cap. At first it was to be just the two of us, a small and flexible expedition, but later we were joined by thirty-year-old Mick Coffey, a steel erector

50   Looking towards Cerro Pirámide as ice crystals pour down around us about 1,000 feet above
     the main Patagonian Ice Cap

from Wolverhampton, and Ernesto O'Reilly, an Argentinian climber, whom we had met a year earlier hiding under a table lest the local *estancia*-owner should discover he had 'borrowed' one of his sheep. Ernesto was a volatile combination of Spanish, Swedish and Irish blood. With Eric being Welsh, Mick Irish and myself English, Ernesto was to provide the spice for our internationalism – even if the ingredients did sound more like the start of a shaggy-dog story.

To have to carry all our expedition equipment, food and sledges up on to the Ice Cap Plateau seemed like nothing but a lot of unremitting and tedious hard work. Could we *float* instead on to the glacier by parachute? Back in England we sought advice from Eric Shipton, the most famous of Patagonian explorers, who clearly thought it a crazy stunt with little likelihood of success. You don't spend forty-odd years wandering the inhospitable places of the globe without learning a thing or two, and Eric Shipton was quick to see some of the problems that could arise with an air-drop in so remote an area as Patagonia.

All the same, Eric and I had grown attached to the idea, for there was a sense of total commitment about it. Besides, parachuting in would provide a visually startling introduction to the film I wanted to make. Undaunted, we persuaded Mick Coffey that we should all four learn to drop out of an aeroplane, and so I joined the Black Knights Parachute Club and explained my plans to my instructor, Brian Jerstice, who immediately wanted to come with us.

After my first jump I bumped into Don Whillans in a nearby pub. He was curious to know if it had been a frightening experience; climbers, more than anyone, have an innate fear of falling. I explained that my stomach seemed to come up into my mouth for the first couple of seconds as I fell away from the aircraft, waiting for that frail piece of silk above me to open.

'Yup,' he muttered, 'I know what you mean. You'd prefer the parachute to be open *before* you jump out.' He was right. That is exactly what I would have liked during those early jumps.

I made four descents, and so did Mick and Eric. We then felt we were ready. I bought some second-hand parachutes and had them checked out by Brian Jerstice, who told me to send him a postcard from Patagonia. No need to write any message, he said, just a number from one to four to signify how many of the parachutes had worked! It was a great pity, as it turned out, that Brian didn't come with us as he would have liked, for while we were away in South America, he was killed when a new parachute he was testing malfunctioned and his reserve emergency chute became entangled around it.

The three of us flew down to Buenos Aires where we were met by an ecstatic Ernesto. Our good spirits were soon dampened, however, when we learned that an airliner carrying a Uruguayan rugby team had crashed in the North, making pilots extremely nervous about flying the Andes. (Several best-selling first- or second-hand accounts were published alleging cannibalism following the crash, followed by two Hollywood disaster epics.) In any case, all available planes had been diverted to ferry food and supplies to Nicaragua after an earthquake there. Although we did eventually manage to find a pilot willing to take us in, we were then thwarted by the Argentine authorities who refused to grant us permission to fly over the Ice Cap. We might just as well have listened to Eric Shipton! Instead of our two-minute drop-in, there was now no alternative but to face the eighteen days carrying supplies up on to the Ice Cap after all.

At the head of the Electrico River (which flows, aptly enough, down from the Marconi Glacier), we discovered an old stone hut that had been built by a reclusive priest in 1935. This became our base camp while we ferried our gear up on to the ice plateau. By this time we were well behind schedule and Ernesto had to leave us to go back to Buenos Aires to sit some exams.

I was anxious to see how I would fare making what was essentially a non-mountaineering film. The flat Ice Cap would be a complete contrast to the vertical worlds of the Eiger and Cerro Torre. Here the wildlife showed no trace of shyness, for very few humans passed this way. I spent a couple of hours filming an almost tame fox that insisted on sharing our expedition food – to the extent that the fox's share seemed little short of the lion's share. Then there was a hairy armadillo that burrowed up below the groundsheet of one of our food tents, leaving untidy holes in the floor through which many of the tinned stores disappeared. It all made interesting footage, but if it went on, we decided, within a week there would be no stores left to take on to the Ice Cap.

In the river I saw my first torrent duck, which initially I took to be just an ordinary duck hell-bent on suicide. With its outsize webbed feet, this curious bird would swim *up* waterfalls, and then whiz down rapids like an Olympic skier. The young chicks bob around in the white frothy water like so many champagne corks. The torrent duck has a frightening lifestyle and its life expectancy is quite short. Small wonder that the species

51   *above:* The almost tame fox that came to beg food from our camp
52   *below left:* A torrent duck in the swirling waters coming from the Ice Cap
53   *below right:* The pygmy owl of the pampa
54   *overleaf:* Resting on the Ice Cap late one afternoon, with Eric brushing-up his skiing, Cerro Lautaro in the background

is now almost extinct. One evening, I noticed that one of the bushes by my tent seemed to be hooting at me. Closer inspection revealed a pygmy owl. These little creatures normally live in burrows on the pampa. Further up the pecking order were the Andean condors, with their ten-foot wing span. These giants could be seen circling overhead on the warm thermals rising from the plains.

It was a tedious and awkward business manoeuvring our two ten-foot sledges through the crevasses and bollards up on to the ice but, once there, we hoped they would enable us to drag 300 lb each with comparative ease. Just because the authorities had refused permission for us to descend by parachutes didn't mean we should leave them behind. They might make useful sails if the prevailing wind was blowing in our direction.

Our first night on the Marconi Glacier brought a setback. Eric Shipton had told us that the pyramid tent he used on his expeditions weighed 60 lb and could withstand whatever winds that blew. I thought I knew better and had settled on a modern lightweight version of a mere 8 lb, which lasted almost as many seconds. Three of the four poles snapped at the first gust, and we struggled to pin down what was left of the tent with large rocks. A miserable night was spent rolled up in the wreckage. Things were not made any easier when Mick had a nightmare and woke us all up, thrashing around like an enraged chrysalis. Dejected, wet and cold, we retraced our steps the following morning, and were lucky enough to meet a South African expedition. They were able to let us have a spare Whillans' Box. These square-frame tents were designed by Don Whillans to withstand Himalayan storms. Proven on Annapurna and Everest, they ought to be equally efficient here. The South Africans had had trouble importing one from Britain because of trade embargoes, and the version they let us have was a home-made copy. Learning this, Mick immediately rechristened it Spring Bokz, and painted its new name down one side.

Our new Bokz tent was six feet long, and four feet high and wide. It didn't have the luxury of a loo, of course, and Mick was the first to sample the dangers of the spartan conditions outside. Hardly had he dropped his trousers when the icy winds filled them with snow, and delivered him a sharp blast up the backside to boot. The expression on his face was too good to miss and I reached for my camera.

The first night on the Ice Cap proper was spent reminiscing in our Bokz about Eric Shipton's adventures here. He had begun his long association

55   *opposite:* Mick Coffey in all the confusion of equipment that, along with the three of us, had to share this four-by-six-foot tent
56   *overleaf:* Our sledge marks from the previous day, pointing like railway lines to the east

with Patagonia well after passing his fiftieth birthday, an age when many people are thinking of slowing down. Not Shipton. He had persuaded the Chilean Navy to land him from a destroyer on the desolate western coastline. Our goals were in fact very similar to his. We wanted to climb a mysterious active volcano, believed to exist in the region which, before Shipton, no one had precisely mapped.

For years the Indians had found ash on the plains hundreds of miles to the east, but no one really knew where it came from, though legend had it there was a volcano somewhere on the Ice Cap. In 1933 a Dr Reichert, one of the first to venture on to the ice, reported glimpsing a volcanic cone during a lull in a storm, but little notice was taken of him. It was not until Eric Shipton saw the peak in 1960, with vapour pouring from its black vents, that anyone knew for sure that Cerro Lautaro was in fact the mysterious volcano and, clearly, still very much alive. Shipton returned on a later occasion but encountered such bad visibility crossing the Ice Cap that he had the greatest difficulty in finding the elusive peak again, and once he had, enjoyed no fine weather in which to climb it.

The next morning Eric waxed the sledge runners and we set off on the first stage of our journey towards the volcano. All the food had been packed tightly into tin boxes, which although badly damaged on the way in by the gauchos' horses crashing into trees, were still watertight. Each biscuit tin contained enough food for three days – dehydrated meat and vegetables, coffee, tea, sugar, chocolate, a few cigars and a quarter bottle of whisky to enliven the 'Coffey' at night.

Mick Coffey and Eric pulled the heavier sledge, leaving me to follow with the second at my own filming pace. The terrain resembled a flat ocean of ice with ridges and peaks rising above the surface like reefs and islands. The weather was clear and bright, the snow perfect, and towing a sledge was a new and enjoyable experience. The first peak we recognised was that of Cerro Pirámide, which rose 6,000 feet above us, creating a beautiful backdrop for the 'Polar Explorer' filming sequence.

The next day we were up before dawn and could plainly see our sledge marks running back east to the pampa like railway lines distorted by a desert mirage. So began the second of thirty-two days on the ice, harnessed to our heavy sledges, slithering across the plateau for all the world like over-shelled snails. There were days of white-out when the sky and snow froze into a uniform greyness, erasing the horizon. Playing a cassette recorder at night, we were lulled to sleep by the pitiful lament of

57   *above:* Eric digging the snow away from around our Bokz tent in the middle of the Ice Cap
58   *below:* Eric and Mick erecting the Bokz tent about five miles from Cerro Lautaro

Joan Baez singing 'What Have They Done to the Rain?' and 'Blowing in the Wind'. Mick recorded in his diary: 'What a place! You have the wind howling on the outside, and Joan Baez howling on the inside.'

Eventually, when the mists cleared, we saw Cerro Lautaro, Shipton's elusive volcano. Eric took a compass bearing in case it should disappear again, and late that evening we erected our camp a few miles from its base. The volcano had grown from a distant grey speck, glimpsed occasionally through the mist, to a high evil-reeking fortress, looming 7,000 feet above our camp.

Our first attempt at climbing it was abandoned after we became disoriented in a white-out and only just managed to find our Bokz again. By chance, we bumped into one of the ski sticks that Mick had thoughtfully placed at 100-yard intervals away from the tent. Back in camp there was a visitor in the shape of a small finch who had also got lost in the mist. Mick solicitously fed it on margarine laced with brandy, and it was last seen describing an erratic course back towards the pampa.

By 10 am that same morning, the weather had cleared again, and the sulphur fumes belching out of the side of the volcano could be plainly seen – and smelt. The rest of the day was spent drying out clothing and equipment, while Eric wandered around listlessly, annoyed at having been thwarted by a bit of mist.

There was no water as such on the Ice Cap. Whatever was needed had to be melted. To save fuel I tried to reconstitute some of our dried Batchelor's food on plates pressed into the snow. It wasn't very successful, but every little helped.

Our second attempt on Lautaro ended just as ignominiously as the first, arrested this time by vast quantities of yellow ice crystals pouring down the mountainside. It made for spectacular photography, set against Cerro Pirámide in the distance, but little else.

After we had been static for a week, Eric devised a new plan. Starting at midnight, we wound our way through the crevasse-field by torchlight and climbed the lower slopes before the early morning mists appeared. Somehow we managed to avoid falling headlong into any of the crevasses, and by 5 am, with the sky still alive with stars, we were well up the lower flanks. Eric pointed to the east at the red planet of Mars which was now rising, pursued across the Milky Way an hour later by the red disc of the sun. The pictures I took then taught me that film and camera often record events which exposure-meters would have you believe were

59   *above:* Checking the photographic equipment on one of the good days
60   *below:* Mick and Eric collecting our climbing equipment before we set off in darkness for the mountain

out of the question. Warmed by the sun's rays, we picked our way up the cold pink slopes. The ice had been sculpted into the weirdest patterns, billowing cascades of mushroom-like formations which offered plenty of handholds, all very brittle.

At 10,000 feet the smell of the sulphur fumes seeping through the sides of the mountain was nauseating. The snow disappeared and we were confronted with an intimidating cone of warm mud. The summit itself was a raft of ice surrounded by five vents, each pumping out a thin haze of foul gas. We were rewarded, however, with a simply breathtaking view, a 360° panorama encompassing the distant Atlantic to the east across the pampa, and below us, to the west, the fjorded Pacific coastline of Chile, where gales had brought disaster to so many seamen – as the names on the map bear witness: Useless Bay, Desolation Island, Port Famine, Cape Deceit. To the south lay the island first seen by Magellan over four centuries ago, where the naked Indians, braving gales of freezing sleet and snow, fished from fragile canoes, carrying with them at all times their most treasured possession – fire. As Magellan neared the shore, he saw pin-pricks of light studding the beach and named it Tierra del Fuego – Land of Fire. Further south still, lay the unbroken expanse of sea stretching all the way to Antarctica.

Our climb had taken sixteen hours from Camp to summit, bringing us to this rare vantage point. I took several rolls of film and recorded a conversation between Mick and Eric.

'How long have we got to hang about up here being photographed?' Mick was heard to mutter on to the tape. 'I don't want to be in the hot seat when it all goes *Bang*.'

As if in response, the mountain emitted a loud and noxious belch of yellow fumes. Cerro Lautaro had obviously not enjoyed the experience of being climbed. The only people to have been here before us, two Argentinians, reported having almost been turned back before reaching the top by the billowing sulphur fumes, and it is easy to understand why. Eric, Mick and I were luckier than Shipton had been, and from the summit spotted another mountain ten miles to the north, which wasn't marked on the map. We decided to investigate it.

Two days later, leaving our camp intact, the three of us set off downhill on skis. Our technique would not have impressed anyone at a trendy European resort, but here at least there was little chance of bumping into anyone on these expansive slopes. Mick admitted that he had never been

61   *above:* On the flanks of Cerro Mimosa with the noon sun bleaching high in the sky
62   *below:* Eric and Mick on skis heading for our second volcano
63   *overleaf:* Cerro Mimosa, our newly-discovered volcano

on skis before, while I surprised myself by nonchalantly skiing and filming at the same time. It was pure delight. Yet we were constantly aware that a broken leg would not bring a friendly helicopter to whisk us away to a proficient bone-setter, but could easily spell disaster for us all.

We left our skis by an emerald green lake and started plodding up the lower slopes, roped together and moving simultaneously. The mountain itself was guarded by the longest crevasse any of us had ever encountered, spanned by only one fragile snow bridge. Mick crystallised the thoughts of all of us when he observed, 'If that drops while we're up the mountain, we'll be there for good!' At that moment, I noticed a vent emitting steam. Our unknown mountain was another active volcano.

The steep slopes were composed of good firm snow until the summit pyramid was reached. Here a vertical mushroom of soft rotten snow and ice took Eric three-quarters of an hour to climb. The strange technique he had to employ involved thrusting two axes deep into the snow with his arms, and, half-tunnelling, half-climbing, pushing himself in a general upwards direction. It reminded me of a crumbling wedding cake, although Mick thought funeral pyre might be more appropriate. There was no way to avoid it as it overhung on all sides. To the left, the ridge dropped away a few thousand feet, to the right was a huge, bottomless gash of azure blue, a monster of a crevasse. But eventually all three of us were atop the tiny summit plateau, where a new problem occurred to us.

Not being marked on the map, our mountain had no name. Mick wanted to call it after his local pub in Wolverhampton, but Eric had a better idea.

'Let's call it Cerro Mimosa,' he said.

'Mim-what?' inquired Mick.

Eric explained. *Mimosa* was the name of the ship that had brought the Welsh settlers to Patagonia in 1865. Mick and I agreed – we couldn't improve on that; so, brandishing a bottle of brandy which mysteriously appeared from his duvet pocket, Mick proposed a toast. Getting protocol into perspective, he drank first to himself and then to our new volcano. Enthusiastically we echoed his toast. After all, it's not every day you discover, climb *and* christen a volcano.

Our snow bridge was still intact on our return, and darkness found us trudging wearily back up the slopes we had skied down so glibly that morning. By midnight we were coasting down the last couple of miles to our tent in total darkness. Swishing across ice at about 15 mph without being able to see a thing was a sinister ordeal. There were no crevasses this

64   *above:* Mick, Eric and myself on top of Cerro Mimosa
65   *below:* Our bizarre method of travel, utilising our second-hand parachutes

far into the Ice Cap, but it was still very unnerving. Twice I ran over Eric's skis and bumped into him without realising he was so close. There was no world beyond the ice crystals scrunching under one's own skis, such was the isolation. But it was Mick, the ski-novice, who got back to the tent first and started up a brew.

Well satisfied with our two volcanoes, it was time to start the return journey, especially as the food was running low. An inflated parachute tied to our sledge with a length of climbing rope pulled us along at a steady 12 mph. Bizarre it may have looked, but it allowed us to be towed from the sledge like water-skiers. Eric tried to direct the parachute, while Mick was ready with a large breadknife to cut the lines if it threatened to carry our caravan into a crevasse. We had not anticipated anyone being run over by a sledge – pulling them in the normal way, they generally stop when you do – but Mick tripped on his skis and Eric, oblivious of his fall, simply coasted over the top of him. Luckily for Mick, the snow was soft, and he was just pressed firmly into it.

That morning we sailed over the ice for forty miles before the winds changed direction and forced us back to more conventional sledge-hauling. By the time the Viedma Glacier was in sight, the sledges had outlived their usefulness. The stoves too no longer worked, and in any case, there was little food left to cook, so they too were abandoned. All that was of any use now was the exposed film and the cameras. There were a few Mars bars, soaked in paraffin and not very appealing, and so, on empty stomachs, we wandered for two days down the Viedma Glacier back to the pampa.

At the first *estancia* a local gaucho was delighted to sell and cook for us a whole sheep. Having lived for fifty-four days on dehydrated meat, vegetables and soup, the harsh grease of the Patagonian lamb sat heavily on our stomachs, unappeased by the quantities of rough gaucho wine with which it was washed down. To end my film, I set up the camera on a tripod across the barbecue to show the gaucho cooking our *asado*, with Mick and Eric on a log feasting themselves. As I walked into the shot to join them, Mick remarked, 'Who the hell are you? I haven't seen you in this film before!'

5
IN THE FOOTSTEPS OF EDWARD WHYMPER

Climb if you will, but remember that courage and strength are naught without prudence, and that a momentary negligence may destroy the happiness of a lifetime. Do nothing in haste; look well to each step; and from the beginning think what may be the end.
Edward Whymper, Scrambles Amongst the Alps *(written after the Matterhorn disaster, 1865)*

WHEREAS THE EIGER'S NORTH WALL IS FAMOUS – or more properly, infamous – for its dramatic accumulation of disasters spread over its entire history, the Matterhorn is forever remembered for one particular tragedy, one particular day's climbing which became mountaineering history's most famous epic.

The Matterhorn was the last of the major alpine peaks to be scaled, yet within an hour of the triumph of its first ascent in 1865 by Edward Whymper and party, there came a terrible sequel. The rope broke when one man slipped, plunging three Britons and a Swiss mountain guide to their deaths and leaving Whymper with his two other Swiss companions clinging to the mountainside. The first ascent of the Matterhorn is always said to symbolise the end of the Victorian 'Golden Age' of mountaineering.

Over and above its historical significance, however, the Matterhorn is an incredibly elegant mountain. By the Swiss certainly, and indeed by a good many other people as well, it is considered the most beautiful mountain in the world. Photographing the Matterhorn called for a much softer approach than I had employed on the Eiger. I wanted to make a film starting with a reconstruction of the 1865 climb and to capture the Matterhorn as Whymper had seen it.

After our expeditions to Patagonia, Eric Jones and I spent our first

66   *above:* In their Victorian costumes – Eddie Birch (left), Brian Molyneaux (centre) and John Morton, who played Whymper (right), with the stage of the Matterhorn set behind
67   *overleaf:* The Matterhorn in winter

Christmas in England for three years. Neither of us had the inclination or drive to organise another full-scale expedition, but none the less we were both getting slightly itchy feet again. Eric fancied a skiing holiday, and I suggested that we could combine it with a quick trip up the North Face of the Matterhorn! And so, as casually as that, it was decided. Eddie Birch and Brian Molyneaux were recruited, and Harlech Television in Cardiff agreed to back us.

It was the start of a long relationship with Aled Vaughan, the Executive Producer at HTV Wales, who secretly saw himself as an adventurer, even if he didn't actually want to set foot on a mountain. Some years later I was able to persuade him to go on a trek to the Everest Base Camp, but for now, if Mohammed couldn't climb the mountain, then the mountain would be brought back to Mohammed. At least, on celluloid.

The Matterhorn was not in good condition when we arrived in Zermatt in January and put up at the Bahnhof Hotel. Constant Cachin of the Zermatt Tourist Office gave us more practical help and advice than we could have dared to expect, and the German film-maker Martin Schliessler, whom I had first met in Patagonia, put his Cessna aircraft at our disposal for aerial filming. Later he even landed alone by helicopter on the bottom glacier to film us on the first ice slope. Both advised against rushing into a dangerous situation.

While waiting for a break in the weather, we began staging our Whymper reconstruction, which proved to be cold fun. We selected a small cliff that resembled the top of the Matterhorn and dressed Eddie, Brian and an American, John Morton, in Victorian costumes borrowed from the local museum. Eddie Birch took the part of the unfortunate Hadow, the young inexperienced climber who caused the accident. He managed to convey a lasting impression of mountaineering incompetence, unsure in his movements, yet with a smug complacency that eventually gave way to terror. But if it was Eddie who slipped and caused the disaster, it was Brian who fell with real flourish, forcibly throwing himself off his 'Matterhorn' in a way only he could. His years of karate training were put to good use and he was seen kicking and striking the snow as he went down.

John Morton didn't need to draw on any acting ability: he *was* Whymper. At least, in the cable car on the way up, that was what he told an overweight lady tourist curious to know who this climber in homespuns and an outlandish hat could be. 'Oh,' she replied vaguely, 'I thought you were dead.'

As this was to be a low-budget production, with a cast of three to play seven parts, John had to double as Lord Francis Douglas when it came to filming the fall. For realism I insisted on the three men being tied together so that John had little choice but to follow the crazy Englishmen down.

Later, back in Cardiff, Terry Elgar skilfully edited the fall that I had filmed, interweaving it with Gustave Doré's engraving of the accident, finishing with a zip-pan down the whole of the North Face, shot from Martin Schliessler's aeroplane. We decided to print this whole section in sepia to add to the feel of history. It made a truly dramatic start to the programme.

Our own ascent of the Matterhorn almost ended in disaster too, even before we had climbed as far as the Hörnli Hut. Fresh snow obliterated our route and several times I had the camera out filming arctic blizzard conditions. The snow-light constantly changed from white-out to beautiful calendarscapes. Suddenly there was a loud crack and the whole mountainside, bearing Eric with it, started to move, sliding down towards a sheer drop. Only a second beforehand we had debated whether we ought to put on ropes to safeguard against such an occurrence. Now it was too late. Unroped and out of control Eric tumbled and rolled, sometimes visible, sometimes smothered by the huge sheet of fresh snow, towards the edge of a 1,000-foot cliff edge. We may not have been able to see the drop through the heavy blizzard, but it was certainly clear enough in our imaginations. By some quirk of professional fate, the camera had switched itself on a few seconds before Eric fell, but I had the greatest difficulty now following his tumbling figure and keeping him in frame. He frequently vanished in the whiteness of everything.

It all happened so quickly that filming was no more than an automatic reaction. Eric fell for approximately 100 feet and then miraculously got on top of the moving carpet of snow, using his ice axe to slow his rate of descent. He came to a halt on the few rocks jutting out of the whiteness at the brink of the cliff and looked up, shaken but smiling.

We were all sobered by the fall, especially as the path we were on was a simple walking track, frequented in summer by many thousands of tourists. I couldn't help reflecting that on each of my filming expeditions to date, I had witnessed and filmed the only fall of that particular trip. None, as it turned out, ended in disaster, but each had conveyed the same message: we were not acting out romantic fantasies for the cameras. This *was* reality. Mistakes warned us of the constant need for vigilance, and what I happened to catch on film was nothing less than us putting our lives at risk.

We spent that night in the Hörnli Hut, with the wind whipping around the ridge of the Matterhorn and sending horizontal snow to buttress the

walls of the hut. By daybreak the wind had dropped slightly and there was a pale, clear sky. We set off up the ridge, then traversed right, underneath the Matterhorn's North Face. It was still well before sunrise proper and already there were new filming problems. We hadn't gone far before the sluggish cine camera stopped altogether in the intense cold. Its fuses had blown. Since making a film was the main object of the exercise, all we could now do was to make a short reconnaissance of the conditions on the North Face and return, dejected, to the hut, and from there, back down to Zermatt.

It wasn't long before we returned with my old clockwork Bell and Howell camera which wasn't subject to such electrical problems as encountered by taking the Canon out in conditions for which it was never designed. We traversed the plateau below the Matterhorn and up 300 feet to the left of a huge ice cliff. From there it was necessary to cross the flat glacier that meets the North Face. Eric launched himself on to the icefield, some 1,500 feet high, with an axe in each hand and freshly-sharpened crampons. He seemed more at home than the rest of us on the hard brittle water-ice that was covering the whole of the icefield. We were soon suffering acutely from over-tightened calf muscles as this 50° slope demanded we balance constantly on our toes like ballet dancers. Nor was knocking in the ice screws any easy matter since the ice was incredibly hard. Enormous slabs like dinner plates would break away from where Eric was toiling and slide down on to the rest of us.

Progress was very slow. Tip-toeing precariously on my crampons, it took a long time to load each new roll of film into the camera. By 3 pm the light had already begun to fade and we were still some distance from the top of the ice sheet. There was no alternative but to stop and carve out an ice shelf on which to spend the night.

We were all tired out and desperately in need of a brew. Preparing a cup of tea while perched on a 50° ice slope is not easy. This was my job but it required Eddie to hold the stove between his knees. The ledge we had hewn out was only twelve inches deep and about five feet long, just enough to allow us to sit down. We sipped our tea and settled down to an exposed wait for the return of daylight.

Brian snored and was obviously dreaming himself somewhere else for

68   *above left:* My re-enacted fall, from the HTV film
69   *above right:* Unstable snow caused Eric's fall 100 feet down a steep slope
70   *below:* Avalanches from higher up the mountain buried Brian and Eddie
71   *overleaf left:* Brian in the foreground holding the ropes for Eric, higher up the great ice sheet of the North Face
72   *right:* Traversing above the icefield into the centre of the face

he fell off the ledge. His dream lasted a further six inches before he was brought to a halt by his belay rope. Eric didn't take off his boots, thus inviting frostbite. The night was long and cold.

I woke early, stiff and numb. It took us some time to get organised, to put our boots and crampons on and to sort out the ropes and climbing equipment. By 9 am we were off and soon reached the top of our icefield, where a heavy layer of powder snow covered every hold. The mountain was so still I felt if we breathed we would shake off its wintry mantle. Being far more sluggish than the day before, we gained only a few hundred feet before darkness fell again.

Our second night on the mountain was spent on a tiny rocky platform, which only allowed us to park our bottoms with difficulty, leaving our feet dangling over the 1,500-foot drop to the glaciers below. As a filming perch, this proved to be quite rewarding, but it was rather the reverse from the point of view of our survival and mental state. But there was no alternative.

By morning it was snowing heavily and powder snow was avalanching down the mountainside. We couldn't see any distance up the mountain and Zermatt, far below, was obliterated most of the time. However, we could hear the voice of Cachin, who had kindly lent us one of his helicopter rescue radios, informing us that the weather outlook wasn't as bad as it appeared on the face. All the same we were nervous of moving from our precarious perch and decided to sit it out until midday and see if things improved.

We brewed up more tea and I filmed in close-up my companions in adversity. Brian produced facial expressions which ought to have guaranteed him a Hollywood Oscar – frightened, cold, miserable and worried, all at the same time. Complimenting him on his acting, he drily informed me that he wasn't. Eddie sat motionless, allowing me to use a slow shutter speed for stills, and thus ensured that I had good continuity when it came to editing. Three rolls of film and two brews later, I paused to ask him if he were still alive and well. A puff of smoke from his cigarette at least suggested his lungs were still working, although the icicle dangling from his nose looked extraordinarily uncomfortable. Eric – as by now I had come to expect – was useless in close-up. Whatever happened, he always appeared happy and calm. Even though his frozen toes were giving him considerable trouble, he still proposed carrying on. Under these conditions, it was going to take us another two days and he knew full well that such prolonged cold would inevitably bring frostbite.

73   Brian (nearest the camera) gathers our equipment for a nightmare retreat

There was so much spindrift pouring down on top of us that it was only to be expected that the camera would suffer. On the film, it is possible to see ice actually moving around in the gate of the camera. Filming with one hand and stirring the tea with the other produced a bizarre shot with my wide-angle lens. One was left wondering how many hands and how many people there were on this meagre ledge.

The weather did not improve at all as the morning wore on. By midday there was nothing else for it but to set off downwards yet again. It took the rest of the afternoon to get down, with nowhere on the way where we could stop for a brew, or even take more than a minute's rest. We tied all the ropes together to give us 600 continuous feet, enough to abseil right down to the glacier at the bottom. I volunteered to go last and waited patiently on the ledge as the cries of the others diminished and died in the icy stillness.

From time to time I pulled on the rope to see if there was still someone on the other end. But with such a long length it was impossible to judge properly. Ice crystals whispered past me and seemed to be hinting that I should follow. The rope was tied to a solitary ice screw and this slowly bent under the weight of the descending climbers. I nursed this anchor anxiously as they all left, lest it drag, casting them adrift and marooning me in this icy sea. Each descent took over forty minutes as the knots in the rope had to be threaded through each climber's own karabiner.

Darkness had already crept up on us, an eerie darkness, with no silvery moon to lighten the ice. I kept fingering the screw. Had it worked loose? Would it pull out as I gingerly lowered my weight on to it? By the time I had been stranded on the shelf for over two hours, I was ready to leave whatever the consequences.

With luck the peg held, and, relieved, I joined the other three at last. We moved some few hundred feet away from the bottom of the wall and set about digging an ice cave. Halfway through the task, there was a gigantic whoosh! Snow, which had built up higher on the mountain, was now sliding down on top of us. There must have been many tons of fine powder which dissipated over and around us. Eddie was completely buried, and Brian partially. Eric and I frantically dug away to try and provide them with at least breathing space, and some minutes later unearthed what looked like a mummified Eddie and one very irate, very abominable snowman, Brian. Eric's fears that he had frostbite were growing stronger by the minute as he could no longer feel his feet.

We trudged on to a safer spot and spent the night huddled together. As

74   Eric fighting his way up a moving carpet of hailstones and ⌐

soon as it was light we continued down to Zermatt, where we took Eric at once to see a doctor. He confirmed frostbite and happily offered to amputate the offending toe in the afternoon. Eric, not wishing to put him off his lunch and, in any case being very attached to his toe, declined his services.

It was early June before Eric, Eddie and I climbed back up the icefield again and reached the high point that had cost us three days in the winter. We settled in for the night once more.

As dawn broke we were treated to a spectacular view of vivid purple and orange clouds. They resembled several flying saucers and were, we later learned, characteristic harbingers of violent weather. With joking references to a Martian invasion, we decided to continue upwards, roped together. By afternoon the storm was upon us and we were engulfed in thunder and lightning. Hailstones rolled down the mountain in frenzied waves, stinging exposed flesh, then bouncing on down. The storm was to continue for thirty-six hours and there seemed little difference between conditions now and those on our winter attempt. At its climax, lightning was striking and discharging only a few hundred feet above us. A snow avalanche enveloped us, pushing Eric off the mountain, and still it kept spewing down like an unstaunchable flood.

While Eddie brought up Eric as best he could across this moving carpet, feeling for invisible holds beneath the white foam, I had little else to do but bring out the camera, though it seemed rather pointless to film any of

75 *opposite*: Eddie high up on the Matterhorn in appalling conditions
76 *below*: Eric climbing up to join Eddie and myself tied to one solitary piton

these events as, within minutes, we were surely all going to be swept back to the bottom of the mountain some 4,000 feet below.

Eric was smiling as he joined Eddie and me on our tiny spike and helped to defuse the fearfulness of our situation. Snow was falling thicker than ever and nothing could be seen at all. It was impossible to make a move in any direction. The decision was forced on us to spend the night where we were, tied to the single peg Eddie had knocked in as our belay. I sat to one side of our little needle of rock, Eddie on the other, and we draped our bivouac sack over our heads. Eric squatted on a three-inch-wide ledge some six feet below us. I managed somehow to balance our stove between my left leg and Eddie's right and make a brew. The seriousness of our exposed position brought us close together, and on that tiny perch on the Matterhorn, we tried to remember all the jokes we knew. One started, 'An Englishman, a Welshman and Eddie,' but the punch line was lost.

Throughout the night the build-up of snow was such that it would push any loose stones from higher up the mountain down on top of us, and on several occasions there were thumps on our 'tent' and quite large crashes not very far from us. By morning there was so much snow blanketing us that we had a struggle to shake ourselves clear.

Route-finding was more difficult than ever with rock and ice alike encased in soft, white powder-snow. Eventually we managed to make out one or two landmarks and somehow completed the long traverse right across the top of the mountain by way of steeply-sloping slabs of rock reminiscent of the Traverse of the Gods on the Eiger. An immense drop yawned below and conditions were appalling.

The sun was setting as we reached the top. Paradoxically, it is always something of an *anti*climax to reach a goal, even one like the Matterhorn, for which we had striven so long. There is satisfaction, elation even, but these are more than tempered by acute weariness. There is only one way left to go – and that is down. Descent can be equally, if not more, dangerous than coming up. Defences are low, spirits and strength are sapped, there is no further goal to spur you on. In such circumstances a slip can easily overtake a party. We would not be the first to fall in such a way. This is, after all, exactly what had happened to Whymper's party after the first ascent, with such tragic consequences. If you break the rules, there is rarely a second chance.

We were either more watchful or more fortunate than those hapless Matterhorn pioneers of a century before, and we brought film back to show what it had been like on that gentle Swiss mountain.

77   Eddie and myself on the Italian summit of the Matterhorn

6
CANOEING DOWN THE ROOF OF THE WORLD

A film is rather like a memory; you make it reflect the way you would have preferred events to have happened.

THYANGBOCHE MONASTERY is almost as sacred to climbers as it is to the Buddhist monks who live there. Huddled beneath the highest peaks of the Himalaya, it has long occupied a unique position in the history of Everest. Since Hunt's expedition of 1953, climbers have spent days there, acclimatising, as the Sherpas made the prayer wheels spin for a safe return. Eric Jones was leading our party through Thyangboche to the great Khumbu Glacier and Everest Base Camp. But we were not there for an ascent. For this unusual expedition, the aim was a *descent*, and one which had never before been undertaken.

Up there, where the snows from Everest avalanche into the Western Cwm, and grind slowly down the huge Icefall, lies the source of the highest river in the world, the Dudh Kosi. Having climbed to a height of almost 18,000 feet, six Olympic-class canoeists with some outstanding voyages to their credit, including a 220-mile descent of the Blue Nile and a shoot of the Colorado River through the Grand Canyon, were to attempt a world altitude record for canoeing, before beginning their descent of the Dudh Kosi, turbulent at the end of the monsoon. They would drop 13,000 feet in the first fifty miles, and then more gently for a further fifty miles to where the Dudh Kosi joins the Sun Kosi to become wide and peaceful as it flows on down to the Bay of Bengal, a thousand miles away. River of Milk is what the name Dudh Kosi means, indicating its milky colour which, along with its cold, it collects from the moraine dusts of the Khumbu Icefall.

78   Nepalese villagers as the sun broke through the heavy cloud

It had all begun so casually. No sooner had he introduced himself over the phone than Mike Jones was posing the question. Would I like to film him canoeing down Everest? Rising to his enthusiasm, I replied that it was the goal of my life. 'Right,' he said, 'I'll call round.' And rang off. Not long afterwards he arrived with his friend Mick Hopkinson, who bore a striking resemblance to a youthful Charles Bronson. On top of their car was a battered canoe with the front eighteen inches missing. Mike Jones, who turned out to be a 25-year-old doctor from Birmingham, had reversed into a lamp post. I could only hope, as I listened to his plan, that he was more adroit at steering canoes. For his idea was ambitious, though simple enough, and certainly exciting.

With film festival prizes beginning to flow in for my Matterhorn project, it didn't take long to persuade Aled Vaughan of HTV Wales that a boat trip on Everest could make a good follow-up. The rest was mere detail. I little thought then of the sheer scale of the undertaking, or of the dramatic adventures that might – and did – befall us, let alone that the resulting film would receive more awards (fifteen in all) than any other I have made, before or since.

In the event, the expedition took some eighteen months to organise. Mike Jones would be leader and my old friend Eric Jones, with assistance from Geoff Tabbner who was very good at arranging things and had previous Himalayan experience, was to provide the climbing expertise. There were in all six canoeists in the party, as well as John Gosling, a Post Office catering manager, who proved an inspired choice for company cook. In case I fell in the river, HTV thoughtfully sent along another cameraman, Mike Reynolds, who may have looked unfit but was certainly not to be outdone by more slender mortals. Growing restive at my long absences in inaccessible places, my girlfriend Barbara was determined this time to come along as well. Geoff's wife Joyce made up the party that finally set out in late July from my home at Old Sodbury, near Bristol, for the 7,500-mile overland journey to Nepal. The most precious part of the enormous cargo of stores and equipment they took was the eleven hand-made racing kayaks which Mike Jones would not allow to be transported except under his personal supervision. I was to fly direct to Kathmandu with all the camera equipment.

It had seemed essential to me to have underwater cameras fitted to the canoes if the viewer was to be given a dramatic first-hand impression of paddling in fast-flowing water. Harry Houghton of Aquasnap made a very neat little watertight housing for my miniature Bell and Howell, which Ian Phillips, an electronics wizard, had gutted and fitted with all sorts of integrated circuits and transistors. I also had an underwater

housing made for the Canon Scoopic camera. The canoeists were sceptical that these would record anything but white bubbly foam but decided to humour me. Being humoured is one thing; being proved right is altogether more delicious. For my frail box of tricks was to show, as nothing else could, the extraordinary beauty and the hazards of negotiating the awe-inspiring cascades of the Dudh Kosi in full flood.

It was not until we set off on the eighty-mile trek, east from Kathmandu to the Dudh Kosi, that I got to know the other canoeists, all bachelors. I was told that John Liddle, a chartered accountant, couldn't help his accent because he had been sent to public school. Rushing to his support, I exclaimed that so too had I, but my flat Lancashire cadence didn't seem to help his case, so I shut up. His canoeing resembled the way he drove rally cars – untouchable when given the right fuel rating, but apt to splutter when not properly tuned. Bradford-born Roger Huyton was always happiest at mealtimes, though his perpetual broad grin made it unthinkable that he could ever be less than happy. Rob Hastings, a teacher, was the thinker of the group, always analysing problems in advance. At twenty-two, Dave Manby was the Benjamin of the expedition, the eternal student. It was hard to figure out if he was an intellectual

79   *opposite above:* Mike Jones, taken from the front of his canoe
80   *opposite below:* The underwater camera housings
81   *below:* On the walk-in to Everest most of the paths became monsoon rivers

scatterbrain or a muddled genius. Mick Hopkinson, also from Yorkshire, was at twenty-eight the oldest and strongest member of the team.

To the river's source from Kathmandu is 130 miles, up and down gradients amounting to 45,000 feet, beginning in rain-soaked jungle, where your T-shirt, shorts and pumps are constantly saturated and legions of blood-sucking leeches feed well at your expense, and ending on the icy slopes of Khumbu.

My first encounter with a leech gave me third-degree burns. Not what one might expect perhaps, but it came about because in my abhorrent panic when the odious creature settled on me, I grabbed Barbara's cigarette and stabbed at it in a frenzy with the red-hot end. The leech left to look for somewhere cooler.

We needed about sixty porters in all, and ours varied in age from fourteen to forty, each carrying a load weighing up to 50 lb or more, for which they were paid about a pound a day. Those who carried the canoes were given an extra five rupees a day for they are as long and awkward as crevasse ladders, which traditionally pay extra. The more alert porters carried the boats upside-down over their heads, which not only kept off some of the rain, but also prevented them growing heavy with water.

The day's march would begin at 6 am, for by 9 o'clock it would be getting very warm and by 2 pm raining. In every village through which we passed, children would come out, oblivious of the downpour, to stare in wonderment at these strange new Everesters. Some nights we would camp in paddy fields, others in temples or barns or cowsheds. Buffaloes made a welcome change from leeches as bedfellows.

As each day's march drew to a close, and tired legs became more hesitant and loads more cumbersome, everyone looked for the camp-fire smoke. For the porters this meant delicious roast chickens, rice, dal and chapatis; the best the sahibs could hope for was dried foods delicately flavoured with fibre-glass bonding resin, which seemed to have pervaded everything. Even our Mars bars were tainted. Local dal and rice became craved luxuries until, after a week, we could stand it no longer and were pleading with the porters to be allowed to share their food. It was not long before dysentery struck, first one then another of the canoeing party.

After eight days we had our first sight of the Dudh Kosi at the Hillary Bridge. The Nepalese have a healthy dislike of water and a real fear of crossing bridges, which are left in disrepair until they fall down – as often as not collapsing while someone is crossing.

82   *above*: Mike Jones protecting me from the monsoon as I filmed the walk-in, while Barbara
was ready armed with cigarettes should I be attacked by leeches
83   *below*: The expedition cooks

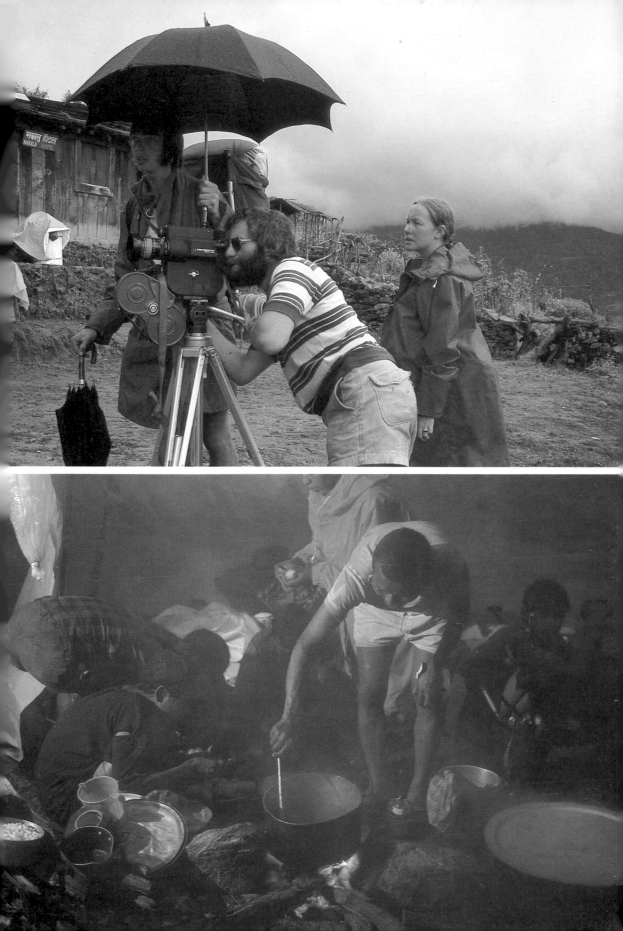

The canoeists were all eager to test these fast-flowing waters at once. Camped along the river bank, we spent that evening watching five boats being paddled frantically down what seemed a very dangerous stretch of water. Mike Jones and Mick Hopkinson collided violently, almost tipping themselves out into the rush of water. Lungs gasped at sudden movements in the rarefied air, and the 'Grade 6' water (the most difficult there is) was falling 270 feet per mile, about four times as fast as anything encountered before. It was a humbling experience.

Four days later we arrived in Namche Bazar, Sherpa country, and on the fourteenth day reached Pheriche. What could or could not be paddled had by now become the main topic of our conversation. Thirty-foot waterfalls were out of the question, and it would be useful to remember around which bends they were lurking. We were three days behind schedule and Mike Jones was a little concerned that the monsoon was coming to an end. In a matter of days a raging torrent can be reduced to little more than a trickle. We were still at least three days' hard walking from the Khumbu Icefall and presumably another two days' canoeing back down. But at our present height, the river did not offer a prospect of more than intermittent paddling. A compromise had to be reached.

It was then that we decided to split the party. Eric Jones would take Mick Hopkinson and Mike Jones to the Everest Base Camp and the source of the Dudh Kosi. Mike Reynolds would go with them and film their descent. Meanwhile, the rest of the canoeists would stay with Geoff and me and concentrate on the more turbulent part of the river, starting here at Pheriche.

To the amazement of Sherpas assisting an American team up Everest, Eric arrived at their Base Camp three days later with two dejected canoeists and an even more distraught cameraman. Perhaps the porters could be forgiven for complaining as they had left any footwear they owned behind and the glacier was very cold. But Mike Jones – a doctor – might have been expected to take better care of himself. He suffered not only altitude sickness but also snow blindness. After briefly paddling his canoe around the Khumbu icebergs, he was attacked by piles as well, for his backside was separated from the freezing Everest waters by a mere 3 mm of fibre-glass. Still, by launching their boats at 17,500 feet a world altitude record had been established.

84   *opposite above*: The two Mikes as their canoes collided
85   *below*: It was often difficult to film as canoeists bobbed past, more often than not upside-down
86   *overleaf*: Mike Jones (right) and Mick Hopkinson paddling around the frozen waters of the Khumbu Icefall

Meanwhile at Pheriche, Rob Hastings and Dave Manby were discovering the alarming effect high altitude can have on handling a canoe in raging white waters. The effort required was akin to that of sprint-running. Dave's canoe rolled over three times and partly filled with water before he abandoned it. Rob, who was further downstream, saw his predicament and tried to grab him as he swept past. At the last moment, he managed to get hold of Dave's life-jacket and haul him shivering to the bank. White-faced, Dave was bundled into a dry sweater, mumbling almost inaudibly for a cigarette. With the river running at a depth of only three feet, Dave's near-miss signalled a warning not to be ignored. When your feet are swept from under you, it becomes impossible to swim in such a bubbling torrent, and fate is all you are left with.

Battered beyond repair, Dave's split canoe was handed over to the Thyangboche monks, where it was eagerly converted into a streamlined chicken hutch. Twelve feet long and weighing less than 30 lb, these canoes had been specially reinforced to withstand the hammering from rocks in the river as well as the sheer hydraulic force of the water. Even so, they could not take all the battering they were to get. Canoe design is really an uneasy compromise between strength and weight. Had these canoes been made of steel, they might have fared better, but would have lost much of their manoeuvrability in the fast-moving river. Perhaps even more important, the porters would have been unable to carry them.

Next morning the magnificent South Face of Lhotse, the sister peak to Everest, appeared out of the swirling cloud. This was where the real river was said to begin. From here, every mile passed downstream would see the river increase in volume as more and more small tributaries swelled the torrent.

Now it was the turn of Roger Huyton and John Liddle to take to the water. Still weak from dysentery, John was soon in trouble. It was enough to confirm that only the fittest should attempt any form of paddling. Rob Hastings was in the best shape and even he was soon struggling to salvage the two halves of his canoe which had been split apart by a submerged boulder, giving him less than ten seconds in which to get to the bank. For a change, the fibre-glass repair kit came in useful, though the stench turned one's stomach and reminded us of our tainted food. Rob, unperturbed, joined the two halves back together on the bank, and carried on down the river.

One essential qualification required of each canoeist was to be able to recover from a capsize by rolling the canoe full circle, every time, and on

87   The South Face of Lhotse

the first try. There may be no time for a second attempt and to lose the boat and try swimming in such conditions could be fatal. Canoeing on this sort of water calls for strength, a well-developed sense of balance, and fine judgment to know when to pause for a rest. Above all, it requires a cool head when situations get out of control, for panic in a canoe drastically reduces the chances of survival, and survival time in such freezing waters can be measured in minutes.

By the time we got to Pangpoche Bridge, the river had entered a deep gorge. Rob wanted to canoe down it as much as I wanted to film it. The danger lay at the other end, where the fifteen-yard-wide river was compressed into a chasm barely one yard across, through which it roared with a noise like hydro-electric turbines. Yet, so long as there were one or two points at which it was possible to break out of the current, Rob felt confident that he could avoid going down the suicidal sluice.

The underwater camera housing was strapped on to his canoe to gain the maximum effect possible. This little camera had a 6 mm Canon VTR lens mounted on it which gave a low-angled, partially submerged view of the river. High above the gorge I signalled for Rob to begin his journey.

None of us was disappointed, watching him pick his way expertly through the boulders, occasionally losing control and rolling over, but always recovering in time for the next hazard. He missed the first breakout eddy as he was swept broadside over a stopper wave, and only just made the second. No one in his right mind would have considered going down the frothy white death-trap at the end of the gorge, and instead we allowed ourselves the filming licence of having Roger vacate his almost written-off canoe, leaving it to do battle with the river gods on its own. The canoe quickly became jammed in the gap between the boulders and was soon smashed to smithereens by tons of water pummelling over it.

Apart from the strain on the lungs sudden physical exertion produces at altitude, the nightmare that continually haunted the canoeist was of being swept out of control for just one second too long and ending irretrievably jammed under a boulder. Even more formidable an obstacle than the whirlpool or waterfall was the 'stopper' wave. The water turns over on itself in a stopper and can seize a canoe and smash it, leaving the swimmer churning until he drowns. The only way to break out is by ploughing through it. This is impossible in full-size life-jackets, making them lethal. The team's jackets allowed some small measure of buoyancy, but not enough to become a trap in a stopper.

88   *above:* Filming from the banks of the Dudh Kosi
89   *below:* Rob Hastings about to disappear again in the milky whiteness

After twenty miles or so the river fell into another steep-sided gorge and under the watchful eye of Geoff Tabbner, Rob surveyed the water by abseiling down ropes in unlikely-looking canoeing attire. Quite a lot of the gorge was navigable, but it was inaccessible except by lowering canoes down from the clifftops and dangling canoeists into their craft. Already we had broken three canoes and there were still eighty miles to go. While I was all in favour of such a spectacular launching, the retrieves would have been almost impossible and an accident here unthinkable. So reluctantly we moved on past the section bordered by Namche Bazar.

If canoes could not be launched down gorges, it occurred to me that I could certainly use to advantage a rope strung across any such chasms that were navigable. I decided to abandon my dry-land perch and resort to mountaineering tactics. By stretching a Tyrolean traverse from clifftop to clifftop, I was able to get clear of the leech-ridden jungle and film high above the canoeists' heads, free of any encumbrances of foliage. The resulting film proved some of the most dramatic obtained on the trip, with shots of swirling white waters viewed through my legs as I swung across the rope.

Down-river from Namche we came to a bridge that straddles another small river – the Bhote Kosi, which was also in full flood, almost doubling the volume of the Dudh Kosi as they merged. The enlarged river made the canoeing more pleasant, but the dangers worse.

I arranged my camera to shoot against the backdrop of an undercut black cave on the far side and then let the canoeists know I was ready. In this sequence of film, you get the impression of stunt-men performing for dramatic effect. When Rob appears, he is paddling backwards and, not to be outdone, Dave bounces sideways on the crests of several waves, appearing to be utterly out of control. What I had not appreciated was that further upstream, out of my camera's range, they had encountered a gigantic whirlpool, just above the fall. The canoeists were not, as it turned out, merely acting for my benefit, but were actually engaged in a desperate struggle to avoid capsizing disastrously. If it had taken them all their skills to get through these 'stoppers', 'haystack waves' and whirlpools, it had been an equally difficult task for me keeping them inside the camera frame, for more often than not they appeared upside-down or covered in white foam.

Mick and Mike had not yet returned from the Everest Base Camp and so we spent some time filming on this particularly violent stretch of water. It was to provide a visual feast. I wanted to get a low-angled view with my

90   *above:* The Tyrolean traverse that I strung across the gorge
91   *below:* Passing the undercut gorge

600 mm lens to give the waves enormous compression. At the same time, the little underwater camera on the canoe would have a 6 mm lens aimed at the paddler. Separated as we were by a distance of approximately a quarter of a mile, the image size of the canoeist seen through the long telephoto lens coincided with the wide-angled lens on the boat. Both cameras were run at seventy-five frames per second, which slowed down movement to make it comprehensible. The 100:1 ratio between the focal lengths of the two cameras created an effect most people had never seen before, and one that was quite breathtaking.

Not content with this, I positioned the Canon Scoopic camera, also in an underwater housing, on the bank at a level that allowed the river to roll over the lens and clear in a matter of seconds. Thundering over rocks, the water shot up to the sky as the canoeists raced past, sometimes right-way up, sometimes submerged, but always down-river.

Having two cameras underwater meant that I had virtually unlimited editing potential to marry film, and was eventually able to create a sequence six minutes long which lifted the film from straight documentary to what some critics have been kind enough to call art.

The 'Everesters' arrived back next morning as we were striking camp. It was alarming to see Mike Jones with cracked lips, sunburnt face, peeling skin and very bloodshot eyes. Yet, after their Eskimo jaunt around the ice floes of Everest, they were more than eager to do some serious canoeing on rapids and contribute properly to the expedition.

The river here curled in a great S, first left, then right, out of sight through the Nepalese forests. Arranging my cameras high on a cliff, I wandered down to the water's edge a few hundred feet below to discuss with Mike Jones, already on the water, exactly what I wanted to cover. Mick Hopkinson, or Hoppy as he was affectionately known, had earlier shot a fifteen-foot waterfall. He made it look all too easy and this may have encouraged him to be over-confident later.

Hoppy and Rob, upstream of us, were coming steadily down the rapids. Suddenly a cry went up that Hoppy was in the water. It was difficult to see more than a few feet upstream but, sure enough, a red life-jacket soon came bobbing towards us. Rob jumped out of his canoe and

92   *opposite:* The Beaulieu plus 10:1 zoom lens taped together with the Bell and Howell, from high above the river where I filmed Hoppy's near-drowning
93   *inset:* Mike Jones on his return from the Everest Base Camp
94   *overleaf left:* The Dudh Kosi in all its fury, with Mike Jones in his canoe and Hoppy just visible on the left
95–102   *overleaf right, reading left to right, top to bottom:* The sequence shows Mike desperately trying to manoeuvre his canoe towards Hoppy, who was continually being bundled down through the waves

tried to grab the body as it swept past, but missed. I felt naked and helpless, especially with my cameras still set up high on the bluff. As the seconds went by, it became obvious that Hoppy was not going to get thrown up on the bank, but propelled on down the centre channel of the river.

I sprinted up through the bushes and trees to where my cameras stood, aimed, focused and ready to roll. The button was pressed before I found the viewfinder, and I immediately zoomed in to Mike Jones's canoe as Hoppy went tumbling past him. All I could do was follow the action through the eye-piece. Time and again he was bundled, out of control, down the river, sometimes with his feet coming out of the top of a stopper, sometimes his head, but all the time less frequently. He tried to get hold of the back of the canoe, but Mike Jones was himself in difficulty, for he was still suffering from snow-blindness and could not see properly beyond the end of his boat.

A little further downstream the river divided round a large boulder, and Hoppy was seen floating down the left-hand side while Mike Jones in his canoe went down the right. On the far side, they seemed to be swept together again just as they disappeared out of sight around the corner. I got the impression that Hoppy had managed to cling to the back of Mike's canoe, but I couldn't be sure. If not, he would be swept further down the river and over some of the larger falls.

I thrust the camera into the arms of one of the porters and raced off in hot pursuit. For the next few minutes, my mind was galloping as fast as my feet, imagining that I had just filmed Hoppy drowning. In a few minutes I would know the worst. I had already mentally decided that if he had drowned, then the film would go straight in the river after him.

People like to see others risking their necks but not actually dying. I wasn't quite sure how to handle myself. I didn't feel guilty exactly, for it wasn't as if I had sacrificed trying to save Mick for the sake of the film. Had I dived into the river, I would only have added to the problems, not being anything like as strong a swimmer as the canoeists themselves. Still, I was shocked and appalled by what was happening, and, yes, the film was definitely going in the river if Hoppy was lost.

Three porters pulled Mick Hopkinson out. He had managed to hang on to the back of Mike's canoe after all, but only just. He was in a state of collapse. Mike Jones, despite his impaired vision, had just performed a classical and extremely skilful canoe rescue on technically difficult waters. Hoppy was lucky to be alive.

When I arrived he was shaking, sipping hot tea and being yanked out of his cold wet clothes. He later explained what had happened in more detail. It had started with a lapse of concentration as he fell under a big stopper which held him trapped upside-down against the rocks. For thirty to forty seconds he had remained trapped until his lungs were on the edge of bursting. Nothing would dislodge the pinned canoe. He had been on the point of giving up when the canoe floated to the surface. Hoppy rapidly parted company with it and was swept down through several more stopper waves. By the time I had turned on the camera on the cliff, he was already in a pretty poor state. From then on, he had virtually given up as yet more stoppers held him under the water, and more water entered his lungs. All he could see was brown and green, with occasional glimpses of blue sky whenever he surfaced.

'I was so exhausted I couldn't even try to swim to the bank,' Hoppy explains in the film. 'I thought that was it . . . the end. I should imagine drowning is very much like going to sleep. I stopped caring, it was as simple as that. There was no panic. Panic involves a certain amount of energy, and I didn't have any energy left at all. I was just passing out. All this time you're rolled along the bottom, getting your head cracked on rocks and things . . . all you can hear is a crashing noise.'

Hoppy goes on to tell how rescue came. 'It's the man in the water's job to get hold of the canoe. Mike couldn't have done a great deal to physically lift me on to the canoe. The water's so difficult he *had* to paddle down it. Once I got hold of the canoe, but I had to let go because we'd dropped into another big stopper, the two of us. If I'd held on, he'd have ended up swimming as well. I was completely exhausted. So much so that just getting hold of the end of his boat was a major effort of will power. Eventually, when he'd pulled me near the bank, I just stared at the bank . . . I don't think a drowning man does clutch at straws. I eventually had to be pulled out by some of the porters.'

Mick recovered after a good night's sleep, and was given the last remaining serviceable canoe, with instructions to look after it this time. It was christened with a felt-tip marker: 'Mick Hopkinson Mark II'.

All the canoeists, Hoppy included, were determined now to go down this same gorge which had so nearly become Hoppy's watery grave. According the river the respect it deserved, they headed off downstream, intent on showing it who was master. As Hoppy said, 'You don't spend eighteen months planning a trip like this and give up just because you fall in the water.' Apart from Dave Manby doing most of it upside-down, there were no other serious incidents.

For ten days they had canoed down from the Khumbu Glacier, each new section of river being thoroughly inspected before attempted. A jammed

103   *overleaf:* Where the Sun Kosi river meets the Dudh Kosi

log across the river reminded them that vigilance was as ever necessary, a moment's negligence could spell disaster. But, at last, the end of the steep section came in sight. They had travelled almost fifty miles and dropped some 13,000 feet, yet they were still only halfway to the Gold River, the Sun Kosi. Food was short and the money was running out. Some members of the expedition were already late for returning to their jobs, or University – or signing on the dole. What canoes were left were in a bad state of repair. At Jubing, Mike Jones and I came to a decision. It was not popular, but it was the only acceptable option open to us.

To have taken the entire expedition along the next fifty miles of river, where there were few proper paths and, in places, thick jungle grew right up to the water's edge, could have occupied several weeks. Instead we made our way as quickly as possible back to Kathmandu. Those with pressing engagements were dispatched for home. The patient porters were warmly thanked and set on their way back to their homes. It was agreed that Mike and Hoppy should do the last fifty miles of canoeing on their own.

They were flown back with two twelve-foot canoes by Captain Emile Wick of Royal Air Nepal to the little airstrip at Lamidamya, perched above the Dudh Kosi, more or less where we had left it. An air reconnaissance of the river on the way was, by previous expedition standards, a luxurious bonus, though the river is much calmer along these lower reaches. The plan was that I should give them three days to paddle down to the Sun Kosi, where I should arrive to collect them by helicopter. It is never easy to arrange air transport when you want it, and even Mike Jones, with his irrepressible optimism, had secretly resigned himself to another long walk back to Kathmandu once the canoeing was over.

With a minimum of equipment and food – a sleeping bag each, a few bars of chocolate and the expedition's last Dundee cake – they set off. There would be no comforting support party on hand to help if they got into trouble now. Round bend after bend they paddled until each curve merged into the next as a solid green wall. Two thoughts filled their minds. Where would they be able to get some cooked food, if only a few chapatis? And where could all those crocodiles be lurking which the Sherpas had said infested this stretch of the river?

It took two days of arguing, cajoling, pleading, to persuade the man at the Royal Nepalese helicopter desk in Kathmandu to pick up the two crazy Englishmen from such a remote spot as the confluence of the Dudh Kosi and Sun Kosi. Eventually the logic of the situation could no longer be denied. They had been flown out specifically to paddle down the river to a point from which there was *no* other ready return transport.

There were four passenger-seats in the Alouette, room enough for both Mike Reynolds and myself to go along but no space for bringing back the canoes. They would have to be abandoned. At the end of an hour's flight, there were two tiny waving figures, evidently relieved to see us and know they were spared the long walk home after two days' wait. But their paddling was not quite over yet. They may have finished their river, now I wanted to finish my film.

Reluctantly the two weary canoeists agreed to paddle upstream for half an hour so that I could get some spiralling aerial shots to record the end of the journey. It was a much-thwarted plan. Having first been blown out of the water by the down-draught from the chopper blades, the two canoeists were obliged to perform the chore three times. The first take was spoiled by my setting the camera at the wrong speed and the second by the sun disappearing behind heavy cloud.

At last it was done, and on the flight back to Kathmandu, Mike Jones's enthusiasm revived. 'Where next?' he asked. It was natural, with a successful expedition completed, to think of funding another on your new-found credibility. But I suspected that Mike was to be disappointed. The world does not want to be inundated with canoeing films, especially after a particularly good one has been made. As it turned out, I am glad I wasn't with Mike the next time he went to the Himalaya.

After a shoestring expedition down the Orinoco in Venezuela and some months as a flying doctor in Australia, Mike organised a trip to the Karakorum. His idea was to canoe down the Braldu, the river which flows from K2, the second highest mountain in the world. It was to end in tragedy. Once more Mike found himself trying to rescue one of his team. This time it was Roger Huyton in trouble. As before, Mike gave chase without thought of the consequences. He managed to drag Roger to the bank, but in doing so, himself slipped down under another stopper. He was swept out into more turbulent water and never seen again.

7
DIVING INTO THE SAHARA

I met a piece of sky dancing
Child's description of a butterfly

MANY GREAT ADVENTURES begin with a simple invitation. 'Come to the South Pole,' someone says, or 'Let's go climb Everest,' or—as in this case—'Let's go ballooning over the Sahara!' No one asks why. The stranger the idea, the more irresistible becomes the challenge.

Our expedition to the Sudan was organised by Mike Kendrick. His team of eight were all close friends, mostly from the Wolverhampton area where Mike, thirty-five, worked as a ballooning entrepreneur.

Aled Vaughan at HTV thought our adventure series might as well encompass ballooning and I went along quite happily with the idea. Up till then I had been on only one balloon flight, a dreamy drift over Abergavenny and the peaceful Welsh border country one misty November morning. I thought then that ballooning could make a very beautiful film, but not necessarily an exciting one. There were mountains in the Sudan, but they hardly matched the Himalayas, and the Nile lacked that certain suddenness of the Dudh Kosi. What there was to offer, however, was a million square miles of empty desert and scrubland, and eternally blue skies. Perhaps, I thought, I could make the ballooning more exciting if I were to jump out of the languid monsters and film them in passing from a 'Ram-Air' parachute.

I had only just taken up parachuting again and it seemed sensible, if I was going to do much in the Sudan, to involve my parachuting instructor, Dave Howerski, in the project – particularly as he already had

above: Dave filmed my descent, with the Nile in the distance

considerable desert experience, spoke fluent Arabic, and would generally make a very useful addition to the expedition. Dave had recently left the SAS to devote *all* his time to jumping out of aircraft.

We arrived in Khartoum a day later than planned and with one essential piece of baggage missing – Dave's kitbag containing his parachuting helmet and camera mount. All things can be found in an Arabian souk if you only look long enough. With my helmet mount as a guide, Dave eventually found an old metal-worker willing to beat a piece of rusty iron into shape. It made a change from beating out Mahdi's original sword for the umpteenth gullible Western tourist.

Returning to the Sudan Hotel with two helmet mounts, one camel saddle and Mahdi's sword, we found that the military escort we had been allocated for the journey had arrived. Under the watchful eye of Major Mahadi, it was to do its best to take us wherever we wanted to go. We made preparations for our drive to Dongola, some 300 miles north across the desert, and arrived at this little village on the banks of the Nile some three days later, dust-caked, hot and weary. The cool Nile waters looked very inviting and I dived in without a single thought for bilharzia, yellow fever or green monkey disease – or yet crocodiles. I wanted to be clean and all these hidden menaces were very far from my thoughts. Once in the water, I saw what looked like a log approaching fast and suddenly remembered all the warnings about swimming in the tropics.

Ferrying the balloons east across the Nile immediately attracted the interest of the local villages. Word spread rapidly. White-man was going to fly in a wicker basket, driven by bottles of gas. The burner which heats the air to lift the balloon makes a noise as it is ignited equivalent to a 1,000-horsepower motor firing without a silencer. As the flames shot up, the effect on a couple of hundred gaping villagers was as dramatic as the sight of their dozens of scattered sandals, abandoned as they fled in panic.

The balloon envelope had been spread out on the ground in preparation for filling it with hot air, and I was horrified to see flames being directed into it with one crew member still inside. Apparently this is a quite normal ritual. The job of the man inside is to manipulate the fabric around the heat-bursts, and he is affectionately known as 'Cremation Charlie'. There is no difficulty in picking him out from the others, he is the one without eyelashes, eyebrows or forelock.

There is another strange ritual that has to be performed, it seems, before

105   *overleaf left*: The Sudanese were very inquisitive as the balloons were inflated
106   *above right*: The balloons were inflated a mile away from the Nile
107   *below right*: The first flight followed the setting sun

a balloon can take off. The balloonists stand in a circle, all talking at once, when one of them stoops down, scoops up a handful of sand, and hurls it into the air. They all stop talking and watch the way the dust settles, then each takes a turn at throwing dirt into the air, debating intently. One supposes, at first, that they are working out the direction in which the balloon will travel, but soon learns that, however the dust falls, balloons have the whimsical habit of going wherever they please.

We finally took off, with Richard Barr and Mike Kendrick in one balloon and Giles Hall and myself in the other. Richard gives the impression of the typical English squire and always manages to look cool and immaculate – except, of course, during landings. There is no one who can keep his poise as a balloon smashes uncontrollably into the ground. Giles might have stepped straight from the world of Bertie Wooster. His charm is legendary. He uses it to best effect in avoiding chores, and positively stars when it comes to persuading others to buy his round of drinks. As a balloonist, he is superb.

We followed the sun across the Nile and watched it gradually sink down over the vast expanse of the Sahara. It was fairly easy for our ground recovery team, led by Chris Beale, to see the direction in which the balloon was heading, but since it could traverse rivers, oases and villages as easily as soft dunes, the rescuers were presented with some difficulties.

We flew until the sun went down, hoping that the wind-speed would drop, as Giles reliably informed me it always did at sundown – adding, at least in Berkshire it did. In the last moments of daylight we bounced along the ground trying to kill off some of the speed. Inside the basket, cameras, film and cameraman were thrown around at random, as all control seemed to be lost. We clung on for dear life. As Giles put it, 'Ballooning is forty minutes of sheer delight, followed by forty seconds of sheer terror.'

At last we came to a juddering halt, and Giles burnt off the last of the propane gas, hoping that our ground party would see the flames against the evening sky. We waited an hour for them to arrive and whisk us back the twenty miles by Landrover to 'civilisation'. As I gazed at the passing golden landscape, my mind went back a few thousand years to the time of the Romans and Pharaohs. Had things changed very much? Apart from a few trucks and the unfortunate clamour of transistor radios, the way of life we saw could have been that of biblical times. The houses were still built basically of mud and straw, with doorless entrances and glassless square holes for windows. The people still wore their traditional *djellabas*, and their food, *akal*, made up as shish kebab and cooked with delicate oriental herbs and spices, was still assisted down with unleavened bread and well-water. How was our civilisation, with its jet planes, television, heart attacks, better than theirs? At that moment, I couldn't see that it was.

In the days that followed, the desert wilderness proved more than a match for modern technology. Our army lorries were continually burrowing into the soft sand like mechanised moles. The balloons were not so hampered, but, as the wind blew only east to west, there was to be a good deal of ferrying overland between flights. We soon opted for the most reliable system of desert transport, the tireless camel.

Hiring camels turned out to be a more involved business than we might have expected. Our balloons were a source of curiosity to the Arab camel-master and first had to be explained in great detail. Then Liz Seward, the only girl on our expedition, caught his eye, and before long was drawn into the negotiations as a bargaining counter. It appeared she was worth twelve camels or 200 goats. Tempting as it was to save ourselves a bit of money, we decided to hang on to Liz, who was, after all, our expedition doctor. Eventually, we settled on a conventional cash arrangement and twelve camels were loaded up with our balloons, baskets and expedition members.

I cannot say camels are my favourite animals. They spit, they snarl, they make horrible grunting noises and would obviously dearly like to trample you into the ground. The habitual arrogant expression they wear, the Arabs reliably informed us, is due to their being the only creatures to know the last verse of the Koran. Riding a camel calls for a broad backside or a small imagination. Dave and I chose to walk.

Strolling ahead of the camel train into the night, the antique solitude of the desert flooded through me. The sands were warm and there was a cool easterly breeze. The sky was studded with stars and only the streaks of sputniks and satellites marked it from when it was studied by the old wise men and soothsayers. What prophecies would they have read from these astral signs? Could they have foretold the possibility of space travel, or of wars in space which could destroy our own world and invade our minds? There was nowhere, I reflected, modern man could go to escape his grim future. All the same, the desert was an invigorating experience for me.

After walking for a few hours, the camel drivers stopped and began to dig what looked like graves. We watched apprehensively, not sure for whom these were meant, and were reassured only when they themselves curled up in the holes and went to sleep. At night the sand retains quite a lot of its heat a foot or so below the surface, and acts like a gigantic electric blanket. Another lesson in desert survival was learnt.

An hour before dawn, the camels were ready to move on, and I positioned myself with camera and tripod at a place where the path of the camels would collide with that of the rising sun. This silhouetted shot of camels on golden sands, with the disc of orange pushing up behind, was as beautiful as it was simple. The sunflare burnt silent shadowy shapes into a jigsaw of light.

Dawn melted into day as our camels meandered through the dunes and windswept hollows. Chameleons pretended to be desert, scorpions lurked under the occasional stone, snakes left furrows traced in the sand. We saw kites circling in the sky, peregrine falcons after prey, and bones bleaching in the hot sun. Nothing was wasted in this harsh but efficient landscape.

After my first bone-shaking landing with Giles, I vowed never again to land inside the balloon basket. Instead, I preferred the idea of strapping on a parachute and making my own way back to earth. This would also mean I could film in safety, and would not be restricted to the basket.

The first time we tried it, Mike Kendrick arranged for Dave Howerski to jump from one balloon while I followed from the second. Although we were separated by about half a mile, I could see him climb on to the edge of the basket, then drop like the proverbial stone. Down and down, faster and faster he accelerated until, finally, after fifteen seconds, his parachute popped open. My instant reaction was that in no way was I going to follow suit. Mike had been rather crafty, however, in forestalling any last-

108   Camels heading out into the desert, silhouetted by the rising sun

minute reluctance on my part by seeing to it that Liz was also in the basket. I didn't want to lose face in front of her, of course, so I clambered reluctantly on to the outside of the basket. There wasn't a proper ledge to stand on and I was very concerned lest I should fall off prematurely. I was to jump on the count of three, but at two, Liz screamed: 'The camera's stopped!' With elbows looped over the basket's edge, my feet dangling in space, I rewound the camera. Then, my nerves almost shattered, I let go.

Falling out of a balloon is a quite different experience from jumping out of an aeroplane. An aircraft has a slipstream which the parachutist can use to control his body movements. Falling from a balloon, it takes a full eight seconds before you develop sufficient air pressure to control your motion. Strangely, you relax instantly. Lacking contact with anything else, you are relative only to yourself. The ground is still too far away to really matter and only the build-up of air rushing past your face gives you any illusion of falling. It is a sensation so pleasant that were it to last for ever, I would not complain. Once at your terminal velocity of 120 mph, you can enjoy flying around the sky by little deflecting movements of your hands and feet. If, after a time, you get 'ground rush', you are too low and should open your parachute immediately. This occurs, strangely, at about 1,000 feet when you would be only five seconds from 'bouncing', should your chute not open.

The chief snag for parachutists jumping from balloons is that of becoming separated. Once we had baled out, the balloon, relieved of our body weight, would shoot up into the air several thousand feet and continue travelling. With only one person left aboard to land the balloon, stray winds could suddenly whisk it up and propel it 500 feet before coming down to repeat the process, like a giant ping-pong ball bouncing across the desert.

We dreamed up one or two interesting jump variations – both for the fun of it and to provide more exciting film material. We worked out various compatible descent-rates for balloon and parachute. One idea was for Dave to leap out of one balloon, open his parachute, and then 'walk' on to the balloon below. This plan had to be abandoned because of the difficulty of keeping two balloons flying close together. We worked out instead 'Mark II'. Dave would drop from one balloon at an altitude of over 12,000 feet, open his parachute and wait for the same balloon to catch him up on his descent. Once the two had levelled out their rates of fall, Dave would then fly into the balloon and scramble abroad. All very fascinating as pub talk back home, but would it work?

A hollow was found in which to inflate the balloons, and once we were airborne, Dave and I prepared to make a double leap out of the same balloon. On the count of three, we let go together, filming each other on the way. Once sufficient air pressure had built up, we flew across to each other and linked up by holding hands. Heaven knows what a watching Bedouin would have made of it. Meanwhile, the balloon shot up into the heavens a few thousand feet.

We repeated the jump, but this time both standing on the edge of the basket and going off in a back-loop. Here was a stranger sensation than ever, for without any air pressure to control our bodies, we simply carried on rotating, back-loop after back-loop! It was only after several seconds that we managed to settle down. Again we linked up in freefall and waltzed the Sudanese skies together.

Most of our flights so far had been carried out in the morning or the late evening, as the balloonists wanted at all costs to avoid the thermals that rise from the hot desert plain during the day. At such times we would relax like normal tourists. One afternoon we wandered around the pyramids of Meroë. Built long after the great Egyptian pyramids, these were the royal tombs of the rulers of Northern Sudan, the Kings and

109 *above left:* Dave (left) and myself do a double exit from the balloon
110 *above right:* A typical balloon landing
111 *below:* Richard Barr, the pilot (left) and Dave Howerski, from outside the basket

Queens of Meroë. The burial chambers themselves were hewn out of the bedrock, then stone pyramids built over them. Stories have come down through the ages of the barbarity of this dynasty. They had one singularly unlovely custom: on the death of a King, all his servants would either be executed or buried alive with him to ensure he had enough staff to care for him in the next world. Should the King be injured, lose a limb or an eye perhaps, then his servants would have their corresponding limbs lopped off, or eyes gouged out. By this simple strategy the King had the satisfaction of knowing that his personal safety was uppermost in the minds of all his servants throughout their lives! None of these precautions, however, prevented the graves from being systematically looted over the centuries, but some of the original carvings, chipped into the stone, have survived intact.

After our escapades in the Baiyuda Desert, we moved south to film in the Dinder Game Reserve, a park roughly the size of Wales. It is east of the Blue Nile and, although we had the approval of the Sudanese government, it brought us uncomfortably close to the turbulent Ethiopian border. Few tourists venture this far from Khartoum and we made our base in a grass-hutted village.

It was disconcerting to find that, although this was a protected game park, quite a few hunters were there, with one intent only: killing animals. The slaughter of wildlife in Africa might be easier to understand if it were chiefly undertaken for food. However, most of it is carried out in the name of greed, with total disregard for either the suffering of the animals or the consequences to the ecology of the area, and is indeed criminal. The days of poison spears or sharpened stakes at the bottom of hidden pits are almost over. Those merely killed individual animals. Horribly, perhaps, since it usually took the victims several days to perish of gangrene. But nowadays there are far more sophisticated and callous methods of slaughter. Imagine a herd of 500 elephants surrounded by poachers, who set fire to the bush and burn them to death in a circle of flame, just to get at the ivory tusks. The smouldering carcasses are left to the vultures. The most that can be got for the ivory of one dead elephant is £10 for a good pair of tusks, and the penalties are harsh. In Kenya, game wardens shoot poachers on sight, but the problem does not diminish. It makes no sense at all. Some poachers even equip themselves with armalite rifles, so that with one push of the button an enormous animal can be extinguished. Another species is helped down the road to extinction.

112   *above:* Ballooning past the pyramids of Meroë
113   *below:* The balloons were inflated amongst the sand dunes

Wishing only to shoot film, we began flying at dawn, when the animals are most active. There wasn't as much game as we had expected, but nevertheless we did see large herds of buffalo and zebra, found where elephants had recently migrated, and were treated to a rare sight of a cheetah running in full flight ahead of us.

I designed the perfect 'camera platform' by attaching a long rope ladder to the top of the balloon, and was able to dangle some twenty-five feet away below the confusion of balloonists, gas pipes and flying instruments. Take-off presented no problems, but the landing was likely to be in a large thorn bush. Flying over the jungle was not as easy as over the desert, and the recovery team often lost sight of us. More care than usual was paid to checking burners and keeping the balloons airborne. No pride before a fall, if we could help it – especially when that fall could land you amidst a pride of lions!

Drifting along noiselessly at treetop height, we could creep up on animals unawares and film without disturbing them. The trouble came when we needed to fire the burners in order to gain altitude, for the roar was enough to frighten most wild beasts. Baboons didn't seem to mind too much, and the hartebeest ignored us completely, but buffalo would stampede in a cloud of dust, and flamingos flew.

Finding clearings in which to land was also difficult and the ignominy of being deposited in the top of a tree was in everybody's mind. If that happened, the basket might simply tip the crew out on to the ground many feet below, like so many ripe coconuts. And because of the scarcity of suitable landing sites, we had to approach at a steep angle, which meant coming down fairly quickly. This could be a bumpy experience and it has been known for someone to fall out at the first bounce and, with the consequent loss of weight, for the balloon then to rise several hundred feet back in the air.

One evening, after spotting a camp-fire a few thousand feet below, I told Richard I would parachute for that and wait for the ground party to collect me. Unfortunately, the man squatting by his fire was not at all pleased to see me floating towards him. On hearing me yell from my canopy about fifty feet above him, 'Hello! I'm English,' he promptly flung his spear at me and fled into the bush. I was so startled that I impaled my canopy on two small trees and landed quite heavily. Only then did I fully realise the stupidity of my actions. I had neither radio nor food, nor anything else apart from one deflated parachute.

After some minutes, with no further spear-throwing, I approached the

114   Shortly after dawn; my rope ladder can be seen hanging from the right-hand side

camp-fire, and with a long torch of elephant grass transferred a light a few hundred yards away. Keeping it alight was more difficult than I had imagined and after a while, I abandoned it. By now it was dark and the jungle was alive with howls, cries and louder noises. Feeling I might be safer up a tree, and trying to remember if the big cats climbed trees, I prepared for an uncomfortable night out. It was quite apparent that nobody – including myself – had any idea where I was, and I felt foolish and not a little frightened. I jumped at every snapping twig, not least when halfway through the night I saw what looked like a lioness sniffing around my parachute canopy. I wasn't sure whether to make a loud noise or remain silent, and still could not remember if I had ever seen a picture of a lion in a tree.

The next morning, utterly parched and quite dejected, I found my way out of the bush, which turned out to be eight miles from the nearest track. There, to my relief, I found the search party.

Although our trip was nearing its end, we could not leave the Sudan before Dave Howerski had finally had a go at the manoeuvre we had planned: parachuting back into a balloon from which he had earlier jumped. After one practice flight, it became obvious that the overhang of the balloon canopy might well deflate Dave's parachute *before* he managed to grasp the basket. Once again the rope ladder came into its own, this time hanging from the basket itself, and with me near the bottom as a counterweight. This also gave me the best position for filming.

The balloon took off with Richard and Dave aboard, and with me dangling on the ladder below. This was not the most comfortable of camera platforms, even if it did afford panoramic views. The rise up to 14,500 feet took twenty minutes, most of which was spent trying to get settled. All too soon, Richard yelled that he had 'ripped' the crown of the balloon open, spilling most of our hot air in the process, and that we were descending rapidly. Dave jumped at about 12,000 feet and whooshed past me in freefall, creating a pressure wave I felt throughout my body.

His parachute opened several hundred feet lower and, after a few minutes, we had almost caught up with him. The balloon was alarmingly distorted, descending now at 2,000 feet per minute, which also caused it to spin dramatically. Dave seemed to aim his 'Ram-Air' parachute at me and

115   *opposite:* For Dave's record attempt, I attached the rope ladder directly to the basket
116   *overleaf main picture:* Dave's parachute only a few hundred feet below us
117   *top right:* I was horrified to see Dave so close in my viewfinder
118   *middle right:* Dave flew back aboard Richard's balloon
119   *below right:* The parachute was firmly wrapped around the basket

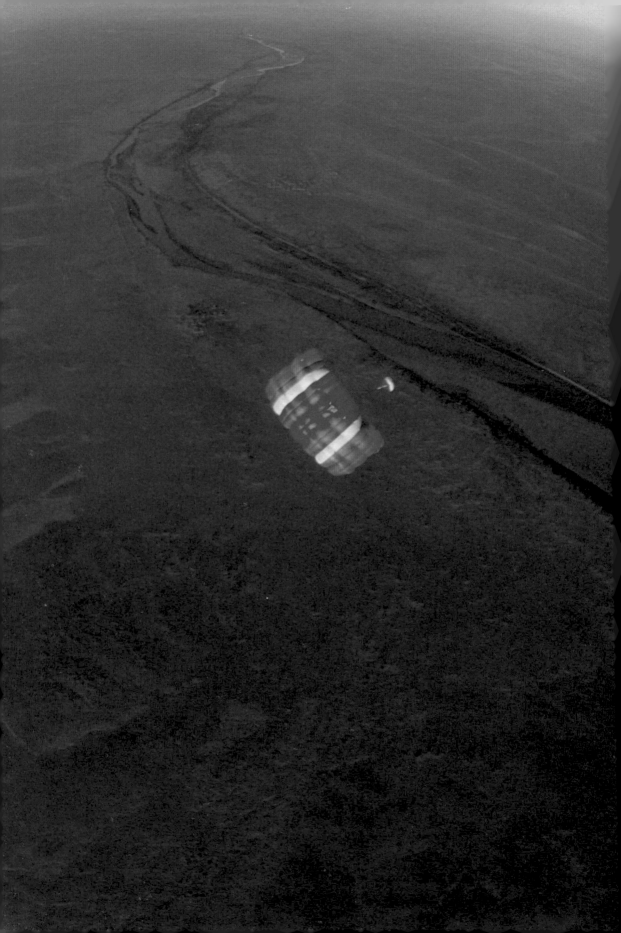

I prepared to take the shock of a 25 mph collision. His first attempt, however, was misjudged and his canopy brushed past. I was filming him with a fisheye lens, yet his parachute completely filled the viewfinder.

By now we were getting dangerously low, close to our agreed cut-off height of 4,000 feet. For Dave it was a question of now or never, and he aimed his parachute once more towards the rope ladder, making for the gap between me and the basket. Without attempting to slow down his parachute, he drove in at full speed. His canopy entwined itself around the basket, while Dave himself hit the ladder at the full 25 mph. The impact knocked me flying, though I was luckily still attached to the rope ladder, and the whole balloon started to spin chaotically. For a full half-minute there was no sound at all from Dave and I wondered if he had been knocked unconscious. It seemed unlikely that he would fall, engulfed as he was in canopy and lines. What in fact he was trying to do was to attach a karabiner from his harness to the rope ladder. Once secured, he looked around and inquired what was happening.

'You've just survived a mid-air collision,' I yelled. 'That SAS training obviously works!'

Richard had by now got both burners blazing in a desperate attempt to slow down our accelerating rate of descent. But Dave had not the strength to climb back into the basket, and Richard was faced with the unenviable prospect of landing a balloon with two people dangling below it at different heights on the same ladder. All things considered, I decided it was time to let go. After doing two back-somersaults, I opened my parachute. It was a great relief to get off that perch and leave the other two to sort out whatever problems remained.

We had crossed the Nile in two places and had been blown about twenty-five miles out into the desert. I could not spot any tracks, or indeed any signs of civilisation at all, and was amazed five minutes after landing to see a bus – or rather a souk truck – heading in my direction. It was hard to tell who was the more amazed. The Arabs had seen the balloon and were under the impression I had fallen out of it accidentally. I managed to persuade them that there was still a pilot aboard, but to explain what had happened to Dave was almost beyond my descriptive powers. Perhaps they thought he had fallen out too, but with Allah on his side had had the good fortune to fall back into the balloon again! After thirty minutes they decided they were running late and, even though they were several days behind schedule, they still had a timetable to stick to. With a lot of shouting and waving, the bus trundled off into the desert.

Alone again in this vast, empty landscape, it seemed wise to make off in the direction of Richard's balloon, which was by then about ten miles away and looked as if it were trying to land. Dusk was falling fast and I could clearly see the flames from its burners against the darkening sky. Could Richard be having some trouble landing with Dave still on the ladder? After walking for an hour with only the moonlight to guide me, I saw headlights approaching. It turned out to be our recovery vehicle, with a very tired Richard on board, and an even more exhausted Dave. Chris Beale had done very well to find us all after the balloon's double crossing of the Nile.

We drove back to camp and, over a late supper, discussed what we had achieved. At first glance it didn't seem to be much. Man's knowledge had scarcely been furthered, yet bringing together those two beautiful flying machines in the skies over the Sudan, two machines that rely simply on natural forces of winds and airstreams for their motion, had proved an exhilarating experience. No amount of technology or computer power would have helped to make corrections in our flight path, our communications system had been limited to hoarse shouts over the desert. We had been in the lap of the gods. From the ground, Dave must have looked like some huge bat-bird, a squawking pterodactyl flying out of the past in search of modern prey. From our balloon, with the sun still warm, he appeared to us as Icarus aloft.

To Major Mahadi's paratroopers we remained an enigma. A hush-hush hit-team, perhaps, planning something murky they had yet to discover. Why else would we, in our crazy flying machines, be performing even crazier flying antics? They could hardly be blamed for their suspicions.

8
DHAULAGIRI, WHITE GODDESS

To decide by one's own judgment the
moment to retreat – that is a satisfying
feeling.
Reinhold Messner

FOR MY PART, Goddess of Knowledge might have been a more apt name
for Dhaulagiri than the White Mountain, which is how it translates from
the Sanskrit. Despite achieving only modest success with our Dhaulagiri
expedition, I learned a great deal from it. More than that, it led directly to
the most ambitious filming adventure I had yet undertaken.

It all began when Eric Jones and I were in Trento for the Film Festival of
1976. We had come to enter my film on climbing the North Face of the
Matterhorn, and if ever there was a case of being in the right place at the
right time, that for me was it.

Our guide and interpreter at the festival was none other than Uschi
Messner, who constantly declared mine to be the most beautifully-made
film in the whole programme. She was so enthusiastic, and so naturally
charming, that any inhibitions we might have felt at being escorted
around by the wife of the world's most famous living climber quickly
melted away. She was quite sure that my film would win the Grand Prix,
no less, and before the official announcements were made, went off to try
to find out if we had indeed been given our due reward.

It was an almost tearful Uschi who returned saying that there had been
'politics' behind the scenes and my film had not won anything! I myself
was not particularly perturbed at the news, but Eric and I had to take
Uschi off for a Martini to cheer *her* up. Halfway through her drink, Uschi
suddenly spluttered, 'But you *must* make a film about Reinhold!'

120   *above:* Shortly before an avalanche poured down from the South Face of Dhaulagiri

Don Whillans had once remarked to me, 'You'd have difficulty making a film about Reinhold Messner. By the time you'd got your camera on to your tripod, he'd be at the top!'

The challenge was intriguing none the less, and I began to wonder where such an event might take place. Uschi smiled and said, 'Why – Everest of course!' Adding, 'Reinhold is going to climb it without oxygen.'

We left Trento that year with no prizes, but with something infinitely more exciting, an invitation to heaven – perhaps literally! When Whillans heard the news he chuckled into his beer mug, 'Oxygen! It won't be oxygen Leo needs to get him up Everest, it will be bloody helium!'

Hardly had we got home before a telegram arrived saying, 'Forget Everest for the time being. I have the most wonderful news – I have permission to climb the South Face of Dhaulagiri and would like you to film that also. See you in Nepal. Regards, Uschi and Reinhold.' Those gossamer threads holding fate together had indeed taken an unexpected twist. From wintry Zermatt and the Matterhorn, Eric and I were now going to Everest by way of Dhaulagiri.

Pokhara has been called the Switzerland of the Himalayas, and it is easy to see why. On clear days the snowy summits of Machapuchare, Annapurna and Dhaulagiri can all be seen reflected in its glassy lake. The trek to Dhaulagiri was to take us ten days, and it was pure delight.

Besides Reinhold Messner, Eric Jones and me, there were three other climbers with us. It was natural enough that Reinhold should have brought along his regular partner, Peter Habeler. They had been friends for many years and as long ago as 1969 had attracted widespread attention with their swift ascents in the Alps and Peruvian Andes. Messner was the powerhouse, the driving force, of the partnership, outspoken and unafraid of public scrutiny. But if Habeler was shyer and quieter, it didn't mean that he was no match for his friend. Like Messner, he had served a long apprenticeship in the mountains, starting when he was a very small boy. Blond and good-looking, he was an impeccable and stylish climber. He came from Mayrhofen in the Austrian Tyrol, where he now worked as a ski-instructor. He was two years older than Reinhold and had once been described by him as being rather like a rocket, more impressive when you light the fuse. The two of them made an astonishingly rapid ascent of the North Face of the Eiger and went to the Karakorum in 1975 where they climbed Hidden Peak in lightweight alpine style. It was the first time an

'eight-thousander' had been tackled by a team as small as two.

Our party was completed by Otto Wiedemann, a young German soldier, and Mike Covington from Colorado, whom Reinhold had met on the top of Mt McKinley. I couldn't help but think that Messner's invitations seemed to be handed out for no more complicated reason than that he had bumped into you on top of some mountain or other – or at the bottom, filming it. He accepted people at their face value. On the other hand, his mountaineering was so serious that you couldn't be sure if your ticket was single or return.

Of the six of us, no two were of the same nationality and, though Reinhold and Peter both speak very good English, there was no language common to us all.

Walking-in beneath the exquisite fishtail of Machapuchare, stopping for game after game of chess, we were a constant source of surprise and amusement to the locals. Here they did not see so many visitors as on the trade route to Everest. Many of our porters, too, had not yet acquired the sophistication of those we had had with us on our Dudh Kosi canoe expedition. They never wore any form of footwear, and draped their bodies in a kind of sackcloth. They were, however, extremely rugged and tough. There was one, bigger than the rest and immensely strong, who habitually carried two or more porter-loads, for which, naturally, he was paid double.

The Sanctuary below Dhaulagiri's South Face does not feature in any of the tourist guides. It seemed unlikely that other Westerners had ventured here before us, especially as there was some quite difficult ice-climbing to negotiate in order to get into one particular gorge on the way. The ice seemed strangely out of place amongst the bushes, grass and trees, and only survived because it was in perpetual shadow. Later in the expedition, a mail-runner set off in high spirits down this gorge towards the lowlands, only to find his path blocked by a bear. Quite understandably, he returned to base camp and insisted on being accompanied. Two mail-runners were enough to persuade the bear that the mail must get through.

On our canoeing trip, I had been disappointed not to encounter my first yeti. I was luckier on the way to Dhaulagiri. Hearing a violent grunting and shrieking in the undergrowth only fifty yards away, I could make out the shape of a dark-brown, hairy creature peering through the trees. It was breaking branches and making a tremendous din. I quickly shinned up a tree for a better view. All I caught sight of was a large ape-like figure

122　*above:* Machapuchare (the Fish's Tail), at sunset
123　*below:* Preparations in a field in Pokhara

lumbering off down the valley. After that I was resolved to go prepared at all times, and would always carry my camera. Even on trips to the expedition loo, I would take a small camera with me, lest I should be caught short by a yeti!

Unlike most Himalayan base camps, ours, although high, was in lush pasture. Above base camp, however, we were obliged to climb steep, snowy slopes and make a long traverse before we could establish the next camp. The first time I went up I suffered badly from altitude sickness, and my misery was compounded by watching Peter Habeler and Otto Wiedemann merrily bounding uphill at an altitude of 16,000 feet. As I bent double over my axe, retching, I heard a tremendous roar and looked up. The whole South Face of Dhaulagiri sheered off and dropped down into a basin out of sight in front of me. The ice-cliff forming this avalanche must have been almost a mile wide. It plunged a clear 6,000 feet before exploding into white death at the bottom. Believing myself to be well clear of danger, as the avalanche had occurred many thousands of feet above and away from me, I continued retching in self-absorbed misery.

Almost two minutes passed before I was struck by an immense pressure of air thrusting against me, followed quickly by so many ice crystals as to blot out the sun. Eric Jones was a few hundred feet above me in an exposed position on the ridge. So strong was the wind-blast that he was left hanging by his fingertips from the ridge for a few seconds, his feet and rucksack streaming behind him. Peter and Otto were hidden in the shelter of a wall of ice. The next thing I knew was that my bare arms were clad in stiff icy armour. Body heat was draining away rapidly, along with all my strength. Furthermore, my lungs were filled with stinging ice particles. My racing mind told me worse was to come. A subconscious fear reminded me of the vacuum effect of such an air-blast, which could suck air from your lungs while at the same time smothering you. Shivering and very frightened, I yet found my finger automatically groping for the button on the cine camera draped around my neck. It must be something akin to the creaking-floorboard reflex which sends reacting fingers to triggers in Wild West saloons. So long as I was shooting film, I felt somehow safe, detached from the action.

The mountain had seemed friendly until that moment, and distinctly unfriendly thereafter.

Camp I was tucked under a buttress of slate-grey rock for protection, and it was occupied for the rest of the expedition. We had constantly to dig out our 'home' as it filled with fresh snow. And ever more constantly,

124   Barefooted porters encounter steep ice and snow in a gorge that rarely caught the sun

we would peer upwards, trying to make out a possible line of weakness through Dhaulagiri's defences.

Eventually, even Reinhold conceded that he had made a mistake in selecting this route. We could never get to the top this way. I suggested that we might at least climb up to the Manapati Plateau, a flat-topped outlier from the ridge running down from the south-west side of Dhaulagiri, for a reconnaissance. Although he doubted it would reveal a more manageable way up the remaining mile of mountain, Messner agreed it would be worth the view.

Reinhold, Otto, Eric and I set off well before dawn. As we toiled up the slopes, the sun gradually warmed us as it rose over the Annapurna range to the east. The ground was steep and very hard in the frozen half-light. I was soon aware that the others had the better of me in technique, and even more noticeably in speed. Still, this was not a race. We were there to have a look and take some film. And for me, it was a new experience to be climbing a Himalayan peak. Anyway, it was assumed by all that Messner should go first – and I last!

By the time we reached the plateau it was midday, and hot. I was surprised to find that I could breathe normally at an altitude of 20,400 feet. I was happy. I had taken some pictures and filmed the magnificent panorama across the Annapurna range. But for the South Face of Dhaulagiri still looming another 6,000 feet above us, we would have felt well and truly atop quite a large mountain. I permitted myself the indulgence of thinking I had, in fact, done quite well!

It would have taken another three weeks to get around to the other side of Dhaulagiri with all our equipment in search of a more feasible route, and our time was running out. I was content with what had been achieved, and Reinhold also seemed to have enjoyed the trip. Back at the hotel in Kathmandu, he assured me that he still wanted me to film him on Everest. Wolfgang Nairz, an Austrian climber and longstanding friend of Reinhold's, was to lead the Everest expedition. It was soon confirmed – we were going to Everest, the dream of dreams.

We tried not to tell the world of our plans, and almost succeeded in leaving the country without any hullabaloo and media fuss. The film we were to make was not for West Germany's ZDF, as the Dhaulagiri one had been, but for HTV Wales. From the excitement it generated in Cardiff afterwards, you might be forgiven for believing it was HTV who eventually climbed the mountain.

125   *above*: On the plateau of Manapati, with Messner on the left and myself on the right
126   *below*: The camp above base had to be continually dug out

For Eric and me, this would be a once-in-a-lifetime venture and it seemed well worth while getting superfit for it. Two weeks' gentle skiing in Zermatt, some aggressive gymnasium work-outs and wallowing in heated swimming-pools soon toned-up muscles and removed pounds. We chose Kilimanjaro in Tanzania for a training climb, not least because of its accessibility, height, and generally unserious nature. I found to my dismay that I was slow to acclimatise, while Eric adjusted to altitude much more quickly. He was able to amble easily to the top while, with rather more difficulty, I shambled back down without finishing the climb. I consoled myself with the thought that I had been higher on Manapati, and remembered the advice Whillans once gave me: 'Why don't you stop rushing around like a mad bugger all the time. One of these days that little heart of yours is going to stop.'

For Everest, I had persuaded Canon in Tokyo to convert their lightest-weight Super-8 cameras to run at the television speed of twenty-five frames per second instead of the normal eighteen. These were also 'winterised' and worked from an external battery worn under a duvet suit. My plan for recording a Messner triumph on film – if indeed that was to be the outcome – was simple. Give *him* the camera! There was no way on earth I could keep up with him, oxygen or no oxygen, and he would just have to film *himself* on the summit.

127   *below:* The summit of Kilimanjaro from an aeroplane at 40,000 feet

9
EVEREST
WITHOUT
OXYGEN

*Happy are those who dream dreams
and are willing to pay the price
to see them come true*

FLYING INTO LUKLA is an experience one would not wish to repeat too often. Its short grass airstrip, clinging to the mountainside, threatens to disgorge unwary aircraft into the Dudh Kosi below. These days Everest expeditions often start from Lukla, situated at 8,000 feet, rather than make the long traditional march-in from the lower foothills.

Eric Jones and I landed at Lukla in the early spring of 1978 and, a couple of hours afterwards, met up with Reinhold Messner and the Austrian expedition on the banks of the Dudh Kosi. I was surprised to see how different the river looked from when I was last here. The year before (when we had been on Dhaulagiri), a huge avalanche had slid down from Ama Dablam into the glacier lake at its foot and created a tidal wave so great that it breached the banks of restraining moraine at the far end. With nothing further to hold them back, millions of tons of water sluiced down into the Dudh Kosi, and the resulting torrent washed away every bridge that was less than ten feet above normal water-level. Miraculously, not a single life was lost. The deluge lasted only twenty minutes, but in that time the course of the river was completely refashioned. It must have been an amazing sight. Had the flood occurred the year Mike Jones and his friends were canoeing down, it would certainly have given them quite a lift as it surged on its way!

Leaving the banks of the Dudh Kosi and passing through Namche Bazar, Eric and I again came to Thyangboche Monastery, where Dave

above: Near Thyangboche Monastery on the walk-in to Everest

Manby's shattered canoe still housed chickens. Near by lived a very old Sherpa named Dawa Tensing who had shown great interest in our canoes when we were last here, and the canoeists and I had spent a memorable evening with him drinking great quantities of *chang*. I explained to Reinhold that Dawa had been on Everest in 1924 when Mallory and Irvine were lost, and he immediately wanted to meet the old man. Dawa Tensing has a face that looks as if it has been carved out of the very rock of Everest. He wears a long white straggly beard and has just one tooth right in the middle of his upper jaw. Taking with us Eric and our liaison officer, Sen, to act as interpreter, we knocked at the door of Dawa's little house. He recognised me immediately and invited us inside.

In the film I was about to make, I wanted to trace the history of Everest and show some of the early material featuring Mallory and Irvine, taken by Captain Noel. What better way than to link up with the past through this old Sherpa, who in Mallory's day had been only a boy. Although he could not remember the actual names 'Mallory' and 'Irvine', Dawa clearly recalled how two young sahibs had set off for the top of Everest and never returned. He thought that they might just possibly have reached the summit, but was quite certain that the fierce winds up there were the reason why they had not come back.

If Messner and Habeler were to be successful this time in reaching the summit of Everest without oxygen, then it would bring the whole story

129   *below left:* Filming with the 1200 mm telephoto lens
130   *below right:* Dawa Tensing
131   *opposite:* The sun rising over the summit of the world
132   *inset left:* Reinhold Messner
133   *inset right:* Peter Habeler

neatly back full circle to those early pioneers: Odell, Somervell, Norton, Mallory and Irvine . . . They would have approved of an ascent without the use of 'English Air', as the Sherpas affectionately called the oxygen bottles. I am quite sure that Mallory would also have been in sympathy with Messner's *by fair means* ethic, by which Messner means, quite simply, giving the mountain a chance. For a man who has climbed well over 2,000 serious alpine routes (and the majority of them solo), who has been to the highest points in all the major continents, and who had, at that time, already scaled three of the world's '8,000-metre' peaks, one could be forgiven for questioning *who* was being fair to *whom*. Weighed against this, however, Messner has lost all his toes through frostbite, his brother was killed climbing with him on Nanga Parbat, and his wife, Uschi, left him because of the time and obsessive love he lavishes on his mountains. Still, in climbing matters, he clearly loads the dice very heavily in his favour, and nothing is allowed to stand in his way.

Installed in Base Camp at over 17,000 feet, and once over the initial altitude headache and dry sore throat, I asked Reinhold to enlarge upon his theories. 'I am quite sure', he said, 'that it is possible to climb Everest without oxygen. Whether it is possible for *me*, at this moment, I don't know. But I know I would be happy enough to get as high as I could and return home without the summit. If this happens, then maybe, in a few years, I will try again – without oxygen. I am not at all interested in climbing Everest using oxygen equipment. So far, I have been three times over 8,000 metres without breathing apparatus and on each of these mountains I felt I could go a little bit higher. I am quite sure it is possible to climb it without oxygen, although I do not know for certain if it will be Peter and I who do it. I think we have about a 50:50 chance, and to a large extent, it depends how we fare on our last high bivouac.'

While maintaining that he would be quite happy not to reach the top, Messner was willing nevertheless to stake everything on the attempt. Peter Habeler, on the other hand, was not so sanguine, and, throughout the expedition, was troubled with doubts. After their first failure, he almost made up his mind to join an oxygen team and repeat the route conventionally. In the end he was 'Messner–ised' and resisted the temptation.

It is important to realise the extent of the debate this non-oxygen attempt provoked. Now that we know they did it, it is easy to accept, but beforehand, Dr Oswald Ölz ('*Bulle*', the bull, as he is more affectionately known), was by no means sure.

'There is no physiological reason', he said, 'why it shouldn't be possible. Everyone who goes above 17,400 feet is subject to high-altitude deterioration due to lack of oxygen. Yet Norton and Somervell reached around 28,000 feet without oxygen, and both lived into old age without brain damage. Now you see Reinhold, who has climbed three 8,000-metre peaks and is still going at an incredible pace – I have the impression his pace is even increasing – and *he* does not appear to have any brain damage. There *will* be a lot of brain damage at high altitude, of course, but of a very unspecific nature. Nine-tenths of the brain's cells are never used by most individuals. These sleeping cells can fulfil the function of destroyed ones. The danger is not to have too many cells destroyed in one area, as this could cause a stroke.'

Bulle clearly had faith in Reinhold, but not all doctors shared his views.

The Khumbu Icefall above Everest Base Camp is one of the most dangerous places on earth. It consists of teetering towers of ice, constantly toppling into the seemingly bottomless crevasses which criss-cross its entire length. It might have been designed by a psychopath to give you even less of a chance than Russian roulette. There seems to be a profound inevitability that someone will be killed as an expedition moves up or down it. Yet never do you expect the casualty to be *you*.

As I made my way up the Icefall, locked in my own thoughts, a loud crack from the Lho La Pass startled me out of my complacency. I was horrified to see a huge ice-cliff tilt outwards, ready to plunge down in the general direction of our party. It was quite pointless to move – and anyway I had the inexplicable feeling that this one hadn't got my name on it. All I could do was to switch on the cine camera and film. The ice powdered past us and smothered Base Camp further down the valley. The Sherpa cookboys in the kitchen were given the instant impression of an early nightfall – or even of their last day.

Further up the Icefall there were ladders spanning crevasses, and all manner of equipment abandoned by earlier expeditions. There was danger, certainly, but beauty too, and it lulled me into hearing only my own heartbeat rather than the creaks and groans of the ice. Some of the crevasses were too wide to cross with a single aluminium ladder, and we were forced to climb down them, across, and up the other side. The Sherpas had all been this way many times before and were utterly fatalistic about the problems and dangers.

Expeditions are fertile ground for forming new relationships and, during the course of this one, I became very close to the Austrian journalist Werner Kopacka, whose satirical sense of humour meshed in completely with my own. Werner decided he should go up the Icefall and report for

134 *overleaf:* Eric Jones and a Sherpa in the Khumbu Icefall

his newspaper, and I persuaded him to accompany me since I had been up several times already and would happily go at his pace. To egg him on, I began teasing him, after we had got a third of the way up, that his stories would win him a Pulitzer prize. Suddenly I realised that I was talking to thin air. Werner had disappeared. It happened so quickly that I didn't see him drop, even though he was only a couple of yards in front of me. The fact that he still had a hangover from drinking too much *Kukri* rum the night before might explain how he came to step off the path and on to a snow-bridge too fragile to take his weight. Peering over the edge of the crevasse, on my hands and knees, I saw a very frightened-looking Werner some fifteen feet down a vice-like crack. He was jammed at the front by his chest, and behind by his sack. More alarming, just below him, the crevasse opened out to a huge chasm that would easily have engulfed St Paul's Cathedral and still have room to spare. Foolishly, we had not brought a climbing rope with us, nor even an axe or crampons.

I yelled to Werner not to move – not to breathe even, if at all possible – while I ran back a couple of hundred yards to a crevasse ladder which had a rope handrail attached to it. Untying knots that were never meant to be undone, I secured a length of rope some twenty-five-feet long and, as I ran back to Werner's crevasse, tied a loop at each end. The loop slipped easily over Werner's head, but not so readily over his shoulders. With the other end of the rope firmly round my waist, I took the strain.

If I had been worried before, it was nothing to what I felt a second or two later. Werner wriggled in the crevasse and slipped, like a seal on an Eskimo's line, further down into the hole. As he slid down, so I was being pulled closer to his icy tomb. Without crampons on my feet, I was unable to stop the slithery progress, and the thought rushed through my mind that we were both going to die. I have to admit that, for one split second, I considered untying the rope. It seemed such a waste, both of us being dragged down to the bottom of the Icefall when one would have been more than enough. The thought quickly fled, however, as I saw a solution to the problem. There was another crevasse some two yards away, running almost parallel to Werner's, and, without a second thought, I leapt into it. Now the rope went from Werner, over the ice-bridge, and into the second crevasse, and we found ourselves in a classic Hoffnung-barrel predicament. As I tried to pull Werner up, I slid further down into my crevasse, and vice versa. We were safe, but it wasn't immediately obvious how I could improve our lot until help came from higher up the Icefall.

135   *above:* Looking past my feet and ice-axe through a crevasse ladder
136   *below:* Werner down his crevasse

Carefully I reached up for my rucksack, which I had cast off in haste before running for the rope, and took out my movie camera. By lowering it on a short cord, I managed to aim it in the general direction of Werner, and then at myself. In my book, it seemed fair to film now that we were in no immediate danger, but just waiting for rescue. We might both grow very cold, but filming our strange cat's-cradle was the only diversion I could conjure up.

The two crevasses met in a V not far off, and by leaning around and stretching as far as possible, I could also take pictures of Werner from the point where our two worlds touched. Eventually, Werner began to grow extremely cold, and I devised a plan whereby I thought he could be extracted. By pulling in any slack rope and wrapping it around my waist, and with Werner putting his feet on one wall (level with his chin) and edging up with his back, I got him to manipulate himself up, like a cork in the neck of a bottle. So long as he didn't lose his footing and slide back down – which he did on a couple of occasions, giving me a few more nasty moments – we were safe. Eventually, peering over the edge of my crevasse, I saw Werner's head slowly but surely emerge from his. Now we had to be careful that as Werner climbed out of his hole, I didn't slip further into mine – or worse, have him join me there. The trick was to extricate ourselves together. We both ended up flat on the ice between the two crevasses.

Werner's eyes, so full of appeal for life, reminded me yet again of a seal, a baby seal this time, stranded on a polar floe. I rummaged in the rucksack and quickly produced a Thermos of tea, which restored the Austrian to life in a matter of moments. As there were no bones broken, I suggested we carry on up the Icefall as planned, but Werner – fairly under-standably – simply invited me to jump back into my crevasse! 'Never – never again!' were his parting words, as he headed downwards and I trudged on up.

We all felt relieved once Camp I was established in the Western Cwm. From here up to Camp II below the South-west Face of Everest, I seemed to be treading familiar ground. Not that I had been here before, but as a small boy I was taken to see the 1953 Everest film and it has remained vividly with me ever since. Like most other mountains, seen from its foot, Everest was remarkably foreshortened. The walls of Nuptse, across the valley, looked much more formidable. The Valley of Silence that lay between the two peaks (so-called by the Swiss expedition of 1952)

137   *opposite:* Crossing a large crevasse by ladder
138   *overleaf:* From Kala Patar the summit of Everest almost seemed to be hiding behind the nearer peak of Nuptse

certainly lived up to its name. The stillness was interrupted only by the occasional small avalanche plopping into the basin below. On clear days, it was possible to make out three old camp-sites on the South-west Face, as well as remnants of tents from last year's Korean expedition when the Lhotse Face came into view above Camp II.

Both Eric Jones and I realised that there was little chance of my attaining the summit on this predominantly Austrian expedition. Even Eric had only an outside chance. With this in mind, I planned for as long as possible to stay as close to Messner and Habeler as politics would allow and film whatever I could see with the naked eye. Armed with my 1200 mm Canon lens and a two-times converter (making an effective focal length of 2400 mm), it seemed to me that little would escape my attention.

As it turned out, I was destined to go only halfway up to Camp III on the Lhotse Face, but I was able to take some very acceptable film of Reinhold and Eric moving up these steep ice slopes. I returned down to Camp II, where I set up my tripod and took a night photograph by illuminating all the tents separately by flash.

That evening the radio crackled out loudly the appalling news that part of the Icefall had collapsed, resulting in many thousands of tons of ice falling on top of one unfortunate Sherpa. No trace of him could be found. I was never quite able to come to terms with the way Sherpas could meekly accept whatever befell them; they were temporarily sad about their lost comrade but, as Buddhists, believed in reincarnation. In forty days a man would return to this world, but I could take no comfort from their belief that it might be as a frog or a snake!

From Camp III the expedition pushed on up to the South Col, where Peter Habeler was forced to turn back with stomach cramps after eating a bad sardine. Reinhold spent the night on the Col with two Sherpas who were convinced they were going to die. Together they endured a nightmare two-day storm, all literally hanging on to the tent to prevent it from being whisked away. Everything this highest mountain in the world could throw at them, it did. Winds built up to 125 mph as the temperature plummeted to −40°F. Eventually the tent started to rip. Without shelter they would all perish, and the Sherpas were desperate for oxygen. Mingma curled up like a kitten and muttered apologetically, 'Power . . . is gone . . .' He didn't expect to survive the night. With Ang Dorje, the other Sherpa, Reinhold struggled out into the storm to put up a second tent, feeling as he did so the first signs of frostbite in his fingertips and nose. As they crawled inside, the two Sherpas came to the conclusion that if they

139   *above*: Camp II, painted by multiple flashes
140   *below*: Evening at Camp II below the South-west Face of Everest

141　Late-evening light with Pumori in the distance

wanted to stay on this planet, they ought to part company with this strange European. And indeed in a lull in the storm at first light, they shot off without further ado, leaving Messner to follow on his own some time later.

When he finally staggered back into Base Camp, Reinhold appeared to be at the end of his physical tether. The little Sony tape-recorder in his pocket played back a voice none of us could recognise. It was his all right, but slow and cracked like an old man's. Yet still his mind clung insanely to the belief that the climb could be accomplished.

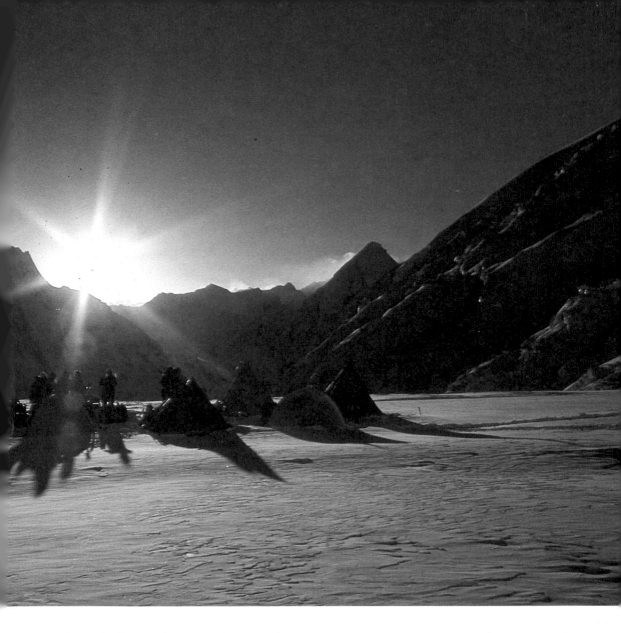

This whole incident was later to have interesting repercussions. The Sherpas felt that their pride had been pricked and they were less co-operative afterwards towards Messner and Habeler and the rest of the Austrians. If they seemed to get on better with Eric and myself, it was probably because we could communicate more easily with them in English, and almost certainly due to the goodwill left by Bonington's South-west Face expedition.

One of the Sherpas persisted in smoking, an unnecessary risk, it seemed to me, in the thin air. When I inquired if it was good for his health, he replied that he had been up to the South Col on three occasions and had always smoked, even up there! Two days after this conversation, when I had returned to Base Camp, we heard over the radio the dreadful news that this particular Sherpa had suffered a stroke on the Lhotse Face.

Though fortunately quite rare, we know from the literature of climbing that such a severe manifestation of acute mountain sickness has occurred in the Himalayas on several occasions before. People sometimes recover, but the poor man in this case remained semi-paralysed. Either thrombosis had resulted from increased viscosity of the blood, due to loss of fluid, or else there had been bleeding in the brain. It was not uncommon, Dr Ölz explained, for climbers examined through an ophthalmoscope after returning from high altitudes to display signs of haemorrhaging in the small vessels of the retina. We can assume that the same bleeding also occurs in the brain. The unfortunate Sherpa must have had severe bleeding on the right-hand side of the brain, for the whole of the left side of his body was paralysed.

The doctors took stock of the Sherpa's condition. He was in a very awkward place – at the top of the Western Cwm – and had to be sledged carefully down to Camp I and then, even more horrifically, down through the Khumbu Icefall. This latter stretch was particularly difficult and took most of one day. By the time they arrived back in Base, bad weather had set in.

No time was lost in trying to help the patient with intravenous fluids, warmth and reassurance. But sadly his condition did not improve much at Base Camp, nor indeed later when he was flown by helicopter to Kathmandu.

This tragic incident was altogether more than Peter Habeler was prepared to take and he went through a difficult period of self-doubt, questioning the whole ethic of 'with' or 'without' oxygen. He tried to join the 'more sensible' members using breathing apparatus, but that did not go down at all well with them. They felt that having made his nest with Messner, he ought either to stay in it or go right to the back of the queue. Peter endured an agonising couple of days. Reinhold assured him that he still believed in him and that it was his choice entirely. If Peter really wanted to join an oxygen party, that was all right with Reinhold – he would not feel let down, but simply go ahead and make a solo attempt – a pronouncement that can have served only to confuse Peter's troubled emotions even more. I almost believe that Messner has the enviable gift of being able to see into the future. He *knew* it was possible, or so it seemed. Peter, a more normal human being, had no such clairvoyant advantage.

142 *above*: Sherpas leaving Camp III on the Lhotse Face
143 *below*: The rescue through the Icefall of the paralysed Sherpa

Once you have committed yourself to the long-term involvement of an expedition, and the wheels are in motion, it becomes increasingly awkward to back out if you begin to feel the decision was wrong. I am acutely aware of this dilemma. Whenever I undertake to film an expedition for someone else, I am laying my whole career on the line. Of course it is possible to withdraw on any given day, but that would mean failure and letting many others down. For me, also, there is always the nagging question of whether I might cease to be invited to film other expeditions in the future. Throughout this Everest climb, as Sherpas fell into crevasses and were killed or maimed, as avalanches poured down on us, as I stopped to think about all those who had lost their lives in the past, trying to gain this elusive summit, I was confronted with many questions which I had to leave unanswered. It was like a trip to the moon, circling it, and returning; once embarked upon, it becomes impossible to turn back, and only destiny knows if you are booked on the return flight.

On 3 May, while Reinhold and Peter were recovering in Base Camp, Wolfgang Nairz, together with Robert Schauer, Horst Bergmann and our Sirdar, Ang Phu, reached the summit of Everest using oxygen plentifully. To carry it they required a caravan of sixteen Sherpas to accompany them to the South Col and above. As Clive James, the *Observer's* TV critic, remarked, 'There is something to be said for man testing himself against the unknown. Where boredom sets in is when man tests himself against the known.' In consideration of their sponsors, expedition leaders often feel an obligation to guarantee success, while at the same time pretending to indulge in the romantic challenge of adventure. An extravagance of Sherpas is something that plays no part in Reinhold Messner's philosophy, as his subsequent expeditions have proved. He has gone so far as to dispense with Sherpas altogether – and even, for that matter, everyone else as well.

Messner feels that a mountain's mystery is quickly exhausted when no rein is placed on technology, when a summit triumph is more important to a mountaineer than self-discovery. A climber who relies on apparatus and drugs, rather than skill, deceives himself. The oxygen mask becomes a barrier between nature and himself, an experience-extinguisher, it muffles his sensual perceptions.

As dawn came up over Everest on 8 May, the day of Reinhold and Peter's

144   *above:* At Base Camp the Sherpa is given medical attention
145   *below:* The triumphant Austrians: (left) Wolfgang Nairz, (centre) Ang Phu, the Sirdar Sherpa who died a few months later climbing Everest for the second time, (right) Robert Schauer

summit climb, I was ready to record history. From Kala Patar a couple of miles away, with 2400 mm of telephoto lens in front of me, I had high hopes of seeing them get to the top. The 'Hillary Step' on the final ridge was plainly visible, but the weather was not to be so kind.

Peter, Reinhold and Eric had gone up to the South Col the day before with three Sherpas, who were to return to Camp III. Reinhold and Peter took over one tent, and Eric the other. Eric had secret hopes of getting to the top himself, and naturally would have liked to do it without oxygen. However, circumstances worked against him. Reinhold and Peter had the good fortune to find extra sleeping bags in the tent they occupied. They spent a very snug night with two down sleeping bags apiece. Eric on the other hand, one man in one tent with one bag, was not so comfortable. With poor circulation, he developed third-degree frostbite in all his toes, precluding any thought of further progress.

That evening was fine, but by morning the tents were covered with sleet. Reinhold and Peter spent two hours dressing and cooking, drinking as much liquid as possible before putting on first their thermal underwear, then a nylon-pile suit, and finally a Whillans eider-down suit. They wore double boots and gaiters covered in insulated neoprene. On their hands they pulled on three pairs of gloves; on their heads, two hats and goggles. Reinhold was to carry with him a short lightweight climbing rope, the Canon AE-1 with 35 mm lens that I had given him, and the Super-8 cine camera to record the summit. He also took his little Sony tape-recorder and of course his altimeter.

The three men were dubious about the weather, as there was only one little patch of blue sky away to the west. Eric decided to wait in his tent on the South Col, in the hope that conditions would improve, while Peter and Reinhold set off to see if they could make any progress up the ridge. They were not optimistic but wanted to test the going. Peter was again indecisive, no doubt thinking of his wife and child. Messner could remember the predicament from his own married life. Since parting from Uschi, however, such decisions came very much easier, especially where personal risk was involved. 'My whole concentration can be focused on coming through – everything before and after plays no part. There is nothing to lose but my own existence.'

The wind was too strong for them to converse except by sign language. When Peter scratched a downward-pointing arrow in the crusted snow to question whether it would not be more prudent to turn back, Reinhold replied with an arrow pointing upwards. After four hours they reached the Austrian fifth camp at 27,900 feet, where they rested and brewed tea for half an hour.

Under the South Summit, Reinhold took out the cine camera and filmed Peter coming towards him. With its battery stuffed deep inside Reinhold's clothing, the little camera worked remarkably well, though at times it gave a false reading on the automatic exposure iris as snow plastered over it.

Then, oblivious to all else, Messner just willed himself towards the highest point on earth where all his dreams focused. At the South Summit the two men stopped to tie on their fifteen yards of rope and advanced slowly along the ridge. So laboured was their breathing that it took all their strength. Every ten or fifteen steps they would sink into the snow to rest before crawling on again. Reinhold forgot who he was, and Peter had the feeling that God had taken over the climbing for him, leaving him free to float alongside, merely an observer.

Messner reached the top first and filmed Peter Habeler coming up the last few feet to join him. This was it. No need to go any further. They had made it. My little camera, which had recorded the event, was cast aside as they hugged one another, sobbing.

146   Peter Habeler nearing the summit of Everest

147   Reinhold Messner by the Chinese survey pole on the summit

After a few minutes, Peter felt a tightening in his fingers, as he had done earlier on the Hillary Step. It might just be cramp – or it might be something far worse. Remembering the Sherpa with thrombosis being dragged half-paralysed down the mountain a few days earlier, Peter grew very uneasy and wanted to set off down. He left Reinhold garbling into his little recorder and relating to the cosmos. At last Reinhold picked up the camera again to bring it back down, proof positive of his journey to the rooftop of the world. He did not feel like carrying the heavy batteries and left them dangling from the Chinese survey pole on top.

Half an hour later, on the South Summit, Reinhold found that Peter had not waited. Further down still, he saw the tracks of a fresh avalanche. Peter, meanwhile, was effecting the swiftest, and cheekiest, descent in history from Camp V to the South Col. Being an expert skier he had started to glissade down the steep slopes and triggered an avalanche that swept him down on the seat of his pants, depositing him on the South Col in a flurry of snow and feathers as his down suit ripped apart.

He lost his goggles, his axe and his crampons, but suffered nothing worse than a bruised ankle. Eric Jones, patiently waiting on the Col, had been silent witness to this strange episode. An hour later they were joined by an equally astonished Messner, delighted to see them both alive and well. Eric made him comfortable and brewed tea, but it was obvious that Messner was suffering snow-blindness. He was to spend the most dreadful night imaginable.

But before the painful ordeal began, elated with success, Reinhold grabbed the radio and could not be persuaded to stop talking. Anxiously awaiting news in Base Camp below, Wolfgang Nairz thought there must be some strange plot afoot when Reinhold radioed down that my batteries were 'plugged into' the Chinese tripod, but it was no more than a private joke between film star and film-maker. All Messner's dreams had come true, he had climbed Everest without oxygen, and returned to tell the tale, even filming himself and Peter on top.

No sooner was the news broadcast than the Sherpas put a damper on the affair. Motivated one supposes by jealousy, they simply would not believe that Reinhold and Peter really had reached the top without using oxygen. Rumours went flying around. They must have carried pocket-sized oxygen cartridges for sniffing on the way, which of course would have been quite futile, since they could never have held enough oxygen to be of any benefit at all. Or, they must have *stolen* oxygen bottles from the South Col Camp. The Sherpas simply could not bring themselves to accept that the two men had an acclimatisation factor superior to their own. In reality, the difference is easily explained. Messner had motivation and a belief in himself, whereas to the average Sherpa, climbing Everest was not so important. It was a lucrative pastime to fit in around the monsoon and the barley harvest.

Still, it later proved that Messner's climb provided them with a motive too. For it was the same two Sherpas who were on the South Col with Messner, Mingma and Ang Dorje, who themselves went to the top of Everest without oxygen in the course of Dr Herrligkoffer's expedition later that same year. Honour was restored all round!

Within three days of the summit climb, Reinhold, Peter and Eric were back in Base Camp. Messner still had snow-blindness, Peter a stiff ankle, and Eric, blackened, frostbitten toes. As we left for home, Messner stayed behind another week to complete dictating his book, *Everest, Expedition to the Ultimate*. He ended his account of the climb with the words:

In the Death Zone success and disaster run as closely together as storm and lull, hot and cold . . . Nowadays I appreciate that – as in all true adventure – the path between the summit and the grave is a very narrow one indeed. That there is no way of telling in advance which way it will finish, doesn't mean that life up on the mountain is any more significant than elsewhere, but it is certainly more intense.

Before we departed, Reinhold wandered over to my tent and with a huge grin showed me a telegram which had arrived while he was high on Everest. It granted permission to Reinhold Messner to attempt Nanga Parbat in Pakistan.

'And who goes with you, Reinhold?' I asked.

'With myself only,' he replied. 'I solo Nanga Parbat. It is my last dream, to make a solo ascent by a new route of an 8,000-metre peak.'

Six weeks later, still high on success, after a brief return to Europe, Messner became the first climber ever to solo an 'eight-thousander'. By a new route, he got to the top of Nanga Parbat, 8,126 metres (26,660 feet), in only three days. An earthquake destroyed part of his route while he was on the mountain and he had to find yet another way down.

The next time I saw him was in Trento, where we entered the film I made about him and won the Golden Gentian Award. There Reinhold told me he now had another dream: to solo Everest. It was to be less than two years before he accomplished that too, quite alone and without oxygen, from the northern side. Before that he had taken part in a successful lightweight assault on K2, the second highest mountain in the world. In ten years he has *eight* times been to the top of an eight-thousander. For my part, I was more than happy just to return from Everest alive, without having a go at the summit. After all, it's a pretty useless piece of rock anyway!

My film, *Everest Unmasked*, was finally ready to be shown on television. In his inimitable way, Clive James cut the whole enterprise down to size in his review in the *Observer* on 15 April 1979:

> *Everest Unmasked* (HTV) started with a question. As the mountain loomed in vision, an awe-fraught voice-over asked: 'Is it possible to climb Everest and stand on its summit without using oxygen? *Even more important*, is it possible to return without brain damage?' The italics are mine. What he should have said, of course, was 'even *less* important'. No importance of any kind can nowadays be attached to the increasingly routine business of climbing Everest ... Star of the new expedition was a German [*sic*] called Reinhold Messner. Insulated against the cold by plastic boots, silk knickers, eiderdown-lined jump suit, three pairs of gloves, two hats and a beard, Reinhold positioned

himself against the pitiless Himalayan skyline and explained why the challenge he was about to face was of crucial significance for the history of the human race. 'It is inneresting to try zis climb whizzout oxychen . . . what is important to explore is myself.' Reinhold forgot to add that exploring Reinhold's self was important mainly to Reinhold. For the rest of us, exploring Reinhold's self was bound to rank fairly low on any conceivable scale of priorities.

. . . Playing strange instruments, monks in lonely monasteries placated the gods. Hoo-woo. Bong. Sherpas loyally fell into crevasses. One of them was crushed to death 150 feet under an ice-fall. Another had to be brought down on a stretcher and sewn back together. Obviously the sheer volume of tourist traffic is tempting the previously sure-footed Sherpas to work hazardously long hours, despite the guidelines laid down by their union, NUTCASE – the Nepalese Union of Trained Climbers Assisting Suicidal Expeditions.

Reinhold made it to the top. But the peril was not over. There was still the danger of brain damage – or, in Reinhold's case, further brain damage. The chances were that this would first manifest itself in the form of burst blood-vessels in the eye-ball, loss of memory, impaired speech functions and the sudden, irrational urge to participate in stupid television programmes. Most of these symptoms duly appeared. Nevertheless Reinhold's achievement could not be gainsaid. He and his friends had proved that it is not enough to risk your neck. It is in the nature of man to risk his brains as well. Fighting his way upwards through drifts of empty beer cans and Kentucky Fried Chicken cartons, Reinhold had added his name to the select few thousand who have conquered the Lonely Mountain.

10

THE SPIDER AND THE FLY

Take nothing but pictures
Leave nothing but footprints
Kill nothing but time

MORE THAN ONCE Eric Jones had declared to me that he intended climbing the North Face of the Eiger solo. He had always enjoyed making difficult ascents alone; indeed, his were the first British solo ascents of the Matterhorn North Face, the Bonatti Pillar on the Dru and the Central Pillar of Brouillard on Mont Blanc.

By 1980, Eric had become a little concerned that he was already forty-three and time was passing rapidly. One day he looked me in the eye and asked bluntly: 'You would tell me, wouldn't you, if you thought I was past it?' My reply was spontaneous. Still holding his gaze, I said: 'At your present rate, you've got a good five years before you even start to grow up!' Growing old is not something that features on Eric's agenda. In the thirteen years that I have known him, he has become less introverted, more openly fun-loving and relaxed. Photographs of him ten years ago scarcely show a younger man than those taken today.

For five successive summers (with the exception of 1978 when he was suffering from frostbite), Eric paid brief visits to Grindelwald to look at conditions. For an Eiger solo he naturally wanted the mountain to be at its best. But the Dudh Kosi canoeing adventure and the trip to Everest with Messner left little time for sitting about in the shadow of the Eiger, waiting for the perfect day on which to set off for the top.

From the outset I had thought what a tremendous film a solo ascent would make, but was unable to see how it could be done. Obviously I could film him setting off, I could even meet him on the summit

148   *above*: Eric Jones on the Eiger summit after making the first British solo ascent

afterwards by going up the gentle West Flank. But what else? I could see no way, however I thought of it, of covering the bulk of the climb without going with him, the one thing precluded if it was to be a true solo assault. Then I heard about a Swiss air rescue pilot who had lowered a guide down to Death Bivouac in the middle of the Eiger's North Face in order to rescue a stranded climber, and immediately I wondered whether he might be persuaded to do it again to enable me to film. The reply came back – yes, he could do that, but Death Bivouac was the only spot on the whole North Face to which he would even consider such a flight, except in emergency conditions.

'Well, what about the West Flank of the Eiger, opposite the Traverse of the Gods?' I asked this pilot. 'Oh, I could almost *land* my helicopter there!' he grinned.

This put a different complexion on things. Eric and I had been inclined to write off the whole possibility of making a film. Now suddenly it had become a reality again, and I was as excited at the prospect of the climb as Eric was. There was now a way for me to get my cameras into some tricky locations without in any way interfering with Eric's lone venture. We only ever discussed two ground rules. The first was that, whenever he decided to try it, I would do my utmost to be available at a moment's notice to fly to Switzerland, and, secondly, that the filming should in no way influence Eric's plans.

Unfortunately the weather in that summer of 1980 did not match up to our revived enthusiasm. Furthermore, it soon transpired that helicopter pilots are simply not allowed to deposit people anywhere in the mountains which might be construed as dangerous without the responsibility being transferred to an authorised guide.

As Swiss law required me to have a guide when I landed to get my Eiger film, and I wasn't going to be allowed to bend any of the rules, I took my plan to Hannes Stähli, who had climbed the North Face with Rudi Kaufmann. These two had also been responsible for the most difficult and dramatic rescue ever performed on the Eiger. Four Spaniards trapped in the Ramp for a period of six days – one with both legs broken – had given up all hope of rescue in the appalling weather conditions that prevailed. Yet, during a half-hour gap in the clouds, these two men had been swung from a helicopter on to an overhanging area of rock to the left of the Ramp and had brought all four climbers safely down. Hannes was happy enough to come with me in less critical circumstances.

By August we were ready. The Tourist Office in Grindelwald had

149 *overleaf left:* Looking down from Death Bivouac to the immense sweep of the Second Icefield. Eric is the tiny dot in the middle.
150 *right:* The isolation of a solo climber

arranged free passes for us on the world's most expensive railway, up the Jungfrau, and Eric had taken the opportunity of running up and down routes on the Mönch and the Jungfrau, the two sisters of the Eiger, just to get acclimatised. It was now a matter of waiting, patiently. Every day we rang the weathermen in Zurich, but did not hear what we wanted until, early one morning, the reply came back: 'Is three days' clear weather of any use to you?' Music to our ears! Eric's response was immediate: 'I will get my gear together and go at midday.'

Eric's minimal equipment had been laid out for three weeks now, and he quickly packed it into his rucksack in the order he expected to need it. Many times we had discussed the pros and cons of certain items. Eric would not be persuaded, for instance, to take a small lightweight sleeping bag made by Pete Hutchinson of Mountain Equipment. It weighed barely 2 lb, and I felt convinced it would more than compensate for the extra burden by allowing him at least some warmth at night. Finally, in response to my incontestable logic – 'You can always throw it away' – Eric agreed to pack it. It was the first hint of unshared anxiety.

When the time came for him to board the train up to the Eigergletscher, a certain dryness came into my throat that was quite unexpected. 'You be careful, Mr Jones,' I said, and turned away so he wouldn't see my eyes watering. This was awful, but worse was to come.

I had always believed in Eric, and that he could do this climb if things went his way; now I seemed less prepared to trust in my belief. One side of me said, 'Persuade him not to go, let's get back home,' and the other said, 'This is ridiculous! He is doing what he wants. You won't stop him now anyway.' I even thought of catching the next train, running up from Alpiglen and lying about the weather. A freak storm or something, I could say. It didn't sound at all convincing, even to me. The train pulled out of the station, with Eric on it, punctual to the minute, 11.58 am.

All my cameras were packed in the back of my car. I was to drive up the road to Mannlichen and telephone for the helicopter when I would first need it later in the afternoon. Through the telescope I had been lent, I followed Eric's progress, this crazy Welshman moving quite quickly up the lower, easier sections of the Eiger. By 4.52 pm he was at the start of the Hinterstoisser Traverse. Eight minutes later he was on the other side and I began to feel optimistic once more.

The helicopter appeared and, armed with one cine and one still camera, I took off towards the North Face. Eric was climbing up steep rocks to the left of the Ice Hose and fixing a rope so that he could repeat the moves more easily at dawn the next day. He waved and looked in complete control of his self-imposed exile from the horizontal world.

Ten minutes later I was back in the hotel at Mannlichen trying to eat a Bratwurst and Rösti. Again I was beset by misgivings: the whole thing seemed wrong and unreal, and I pushed the plate to one side after no more than a couple of mouthfuls. I hadn't realised until now how important Eric's friendship was to me. At this moment I could do nothing to help him. I refused the beer and settled for a cup of lemon tea.

Together with Hannes Stähli, I was to be lowered shortly after dawn the next day on to Death Bivouac to try and film Eric coming across the Second Icefield. I lay awake all night, and long before daybreak was dressed and peering through my telescope at that compulsive North Face. Eric left the Swallow's Nest in the dark, climbed the rope he had fixed the previous evening and by torchlight started up the Second Icefield. Although safer in the cold of the night, climbing in a tiny bubble of light makes you appear vulnerable. At quarter-past six I spotted Eric, a third of the way across the Second Icefield. I couldn't believe it. Even with the naked eye, you could see the tiny moving dot three miles away. I had told Hannes to arrive at seven, but at this rate Eric would get to Death Bivouac before us. Becoming agitated, I woke up the pilot and the winch operator, explaining that we should leave as soon as Hannes turned up. He arrived on the dot of seven; in the same instant, I locked the keys inside my car. Panic. The third member of the helicopter crew, the doctor, operated on the rear window of my car to enable the slimmer winchman to crawl in and retrieve the keys so that I could get out the couple of necessary items I had inadvertently imprisoned inside the boot.

At last we were airborne. Now it was time to worry on my own account. I had quite cheerfully planned to be swung on to a tiny ledge halfway up the most notorious mountain on earth, and left there. Now, as the moment approached, I wasn't quite so sanguine at the prospect. Hannes might have performed similar manoeuvres before, but I hadn't. I was wearing my parachuting helmet with a camera attached to the top and, as ten years earlier on the same mountain, I found it easier to hide behind the camera, concentrate on the filming, and not dwell on other aspects. Hannes was lowered first. Then, all too soon, the helicopter spiralled back. Now it was my turn. As I clipped the hook through the karabiner on my Whillans harness, I felt the cold rush of early-morning air. I didn't look down to the valley 4,000 feet below, as I wanted to keep the camera on my helmet pointing upwards. The winch was very rapid. No sooner, it seemed, was I out of the door than I felt a tug from Hannes, pulling me on to a tiny six-inch-wide ledge just below Death Bivouac. If there exists a more awesome place to swing to at the end of a rope, I cannot envisage it. Next came the dangerous part—unhooking from the helicopter before hooking on to the belay. You cannot be clipped to both.

Ten minutes later we had climbed to Death Bivouac and, while Hannes dug away and flattened the fresh snow, I unpacked my tripod, cameras and lenses. Five minutes after that I was ready, and there was Eric climbing towards us. If I had been anxious for him before at a distance, it was nothing to what I became now, watching him close to. His only rope was coiled over his shoulder and he was moving without any form of protection. I concentrated on the filming. So far, so good. Everything had gone according to plan, and I had filmed him coming across the last 500 feet of the Second Icefield. Then he disappeared from sight below the Flatiron. Time for a brew. Thoughtfully, Hannes had brought along a little stove and melted some snow. I, too, had brought a Thermos of fresh tea for Eric. We were both concerned to quench his thirst, even though we realised such outside help might be construed as improper on a solo ascent.

It was an hour before Eric emerged again, coming up the side of the Flatiron. He had had a problem leaving the Second Icefield in one of the chimneys flanking the buttress, and had almost fallen off in his haste. Watching him now, gently padding his way up the ice-covered rocks, without the umbilical cord of the rope, was unnerving to say the least.

Although the two had spoken on the phone, Eric and Hannes had not actually met.

'Hello, Hannes, I'm Eric.'

'Yes . . . I know . . . pleased to meet you.'

'Would you like some tea?' I chipped in, feeling very British.

'Thank you,' replied Eric.

'What about breakfast? I've brought you two ham sandwiches.'

Jokingly Eric replied, 'It would be unethical . . . I'll have some more tea in a minute,' he compromised, explaining he wasn't really hungry as he was quite wound up inside. For the last ten minutes I had been toying again with the idea of trying to persuade him to give up. Maybe I could get him to come back with us in the helicopter. Then Hannes broke in to inquire if perhaps we had something Eric might have forgotten, equipment or anything.

'A couple of karabiners might be useful, if you could spare them,' was Eric's reply. Hannes and I tried to outdraw each other, but Eric would take only two.

While I had been filming Eric on the Second Icefield, Hannes had cut a small ledge out of the steeper Third Icefield, thirty feet away, so that I could move across to cover Eric moving on. Three-quarters of an hour passed very quickly. Little was said. Conversation was somehow strained

151   A short tea-break at Death Bivouac after completing the Second Icefield

and out of place. Eric was preoccupied thinking about this and his earlier solo climbs. Maybe they had been rash and ill-conceived, but this time he felt a strong rebirth of confidence and was at peace inwardly. I misinterpreted his silence and didn't want to see him go.

With three cameras dangling around my neck, I tiptoed across the Third Icefield to Hannes's little ledge – on the end of a rope, naturally. All too soon, Eric trudged past me upwards and diagonally away across the ice. Luckily he moved fast and my concentration was absorbed in recording him. Even so, when he slipped, my heart thumped. It was a rotten piece of snow covering the ice which had caused his foot to shoot away beneath him, but luckily only one crampon had slipped. The camera didn't have a heart and carried on exposing film. Gaining a better grip, Eric continued across the Third Icefield for about twenty minutes, while I, on my little perch directly below the left-hand leg of the Spider, towering 700 feet above, was feeling somewhat vulnerable without a crash helmet. I gingerly retraced my steps to Death Bivouac on my front points, with cameras clanging.

Once again I set up the tripod in order to get steady shots of Eric moving up the chimneys of the Ramp. I didn't want to call in the helicopter too early for fear it might upset Eric – either physically by its closeness, or mentally when he saw us whisked away, leaving him to it.

The two of us abseiled down the sixty feet to the little ledge we had landed on and, after a while, requested to be collected. Once again I had the helmet-camera running to record this bizarre manoeuvre. Ten minutes later we were drinking tea at Mannlichen. The sense of unreality was growing stronger by the minute.

I joined Hannes and the helicopter crew for a meal, and again tried to force down some food, but without success. Half an hour later, I came out to take another look through the telescope. But I could not find the little moving figure. Visibility was excellent. There seemed no other explanation but that he had fallen. Distraught, I let the telescope range across the face. Then, at quarter-past two, I picked out his yellow helmet, very far away, and my breathing became more normal. I did not know whether Eric was having a good time or bad, but at my end things were certainly not good.

As it happened, Eric was not having things all his own way. Throughout the climb, he was reminded again and again of previous disasters. Here, high in the Ramp, at the place known as the Silver Trench, the very first climber to attempt to solo the Eiger – Adolf Meyr – had fallen nearly 5,000 feet to his death. It was a notoriously difficult section

152   Starting up the 60° Third Icefield

and there were stones falling. Eric, without any protection at all, his crampons failing to find any secure purchase, felt himself go right through the 'fear barrier'. He knew he could fall, but was able to remain unruffled at the prospect. Afterwards he said, 'Fear was an emotion I didn't need. It got in the way. Once it was under control, I felt calmer than I've ever felt in my whole life. I knew that at any second I was likely to slip and fall to my death. Anything I could do to avoid this was a bonus. I'd lost everything – so now I could only gain. It was a strange feeling.'

The next part of the plan was to drop on to the West Flank and film Eric coming across the Traverse of the Gods. On the way, I took one more aerial sequence as Eric moved up the Icefield to the Brittle Ledges. By now it was 6 o'clock, and Hannes and I debated whether or not he would move across the Traverse of the Gods that night, and, if so, where he would end up before darkness overtook him.

By 6.30 it was apparent that he was not going to come into view and the pilot grew anxious to lift us off. Yet a quick detour on the flight back allowed me to film Eric waving from his second bivouac. He looked comfortable, but was sitting on scree-covered ledges; were he to relax for long, he might find himself rolling over the edge. I hoped he was tied on well.

Back in Death Bivouac we had agreed that I should flash my car headlights at 8 o'clock, but when I did so, there was no answering flash from Eric on the face. I felt desolate.

Early the following morning, we took off and regained our larger platform on the West Flank, about 800 feet to the right of the Traverse of the Gods. I started to worry again when Eric failed to appear before 8 am, but he knew the weather forecast was good and didn't want to rush early in the morning when everything was cold. He was no doubt stiff after an awkward night's disturbed sleep. When he did finally emerge in my telephoto lens, I could see him attach his crampons, then move quickly across the Traverse of the Gods. It took him just over an hour.

Now we came to the most critical part of the helicopter exercise. It almost required me to be in two places at once. I wanted to film Eric moving up the first fifty feet of the Spider, after which he would go out of view behind a rock buttress. At this point I needed the helicopter to collect me so that I could get a close-up view from the air as he moved up the White Spider. I summoned the chopper, and back over the radio came the reply that it was moving a dead cow down to Grindelwald! He would be back in ten minutes, I was assured. The speed at which Eric had started up

153–4   *above left and right:* Being lowered with my equipment on to the West Flank of the Eiger
155   *below:* Eric made his second bivouac on the Brittle Ledges at the top of the Ramp

the Spider made me think he would soon be at the top and I should miss
the shot. But, true to his word, Buchardt, the pilot, arrived ten minutes
later, picked me up, and whisked me away round the buttress to film the
final stages of the ascent of the Spider.

I later learned that Eric had been cool enough to remember the plan,
and had waited on a little ledge he had chipped in the ice until he saw the
helicopter. It showed what complete mental control he had, and I was
rewarded with the most dramatic piece of mountaineering film I could
ever imagine. A bird's-eye viewpoint, straight on to the Spider, gives no
impression of the angle of the ice and it appears as a vertical sheet. The
whole Spider took Eric forty minutes from bottom to top, and I was in
ecstasy about the filming. This section looked more precarious than
anything I had yet seen. I just gritted my teeth, pressed the camera button
and hoped he was happy. Eric had always assured me that on pure ice he
was in complete control and would not fall, unless of course he was hit by
a falling stone. If Eric conveyed this message to me, the resulting film does
not. He looks more than anything like a fly on the wall, or more
appropriately in this case, a fly in the Spider's web.

We returned to the West Flank. I waited while Eric climbed the Exit
Cracks at great speed. Through my 800 mm lens, I could pick him out
clearly as he moved competently through the chimneys and iced-up
fissures. I was later to discover that he allowed himself to relax here to an
almost dangerous degree, and had to take a hold of himself on the easier
ground at the top, much more so than lower down where the climbing
was technically more difficult. He knew now he would succeed, but was
tired and could easily have let his concentration lapse.

The helicopter took me back to Mannlichen where there was a further
wait while Eric made his way along the Mittelegi Ridge and so to the top. I
still didn't dare to eat anything, but just gulped down a Coca-Cola. The
crew of the helicopter sat down to a meal, but said they could be ready at a
couple of minutes' notice. Eric, it seemed, did not want to hang around
and could be seen with the naked eye almost running upwards along the
Mittelegi Ridge towards the summit. I rushed into the restaurant and
implored the pilot to finish his Wiener schnitzel and chips and get his
machine airborne.

We arrived at the top simultaneously. Hannes and I, plus cameras, were
winched down. Over the radio had come the news that the helicopter was

156   *opposite:* The white band in the centre is the Traverse of the Gods; Eric can just be seen in the
          middle
157   *inset:* Eric as seen through the Canon 800 mm telephoto lens, taken from the 16 mm film
158   *overleaf left:* Nearing the top of the Spider
159   *right:* The pilot was persuaded to go closer

wanted for a rescue; they said they would come back for us as soon as they could. It didn't matter at all. We had all the time in the world!

It was 3 o'clock in the afternoon when Eric climbed over the last crest. He knelt down in the snow, overcome with emotion. It was about ten minutes before he could speak. There was a lump in my throat. Everything was so quiet. Serene. On top of the Eiger there was no wind, no intrusions of any kind, just this blessed silence. The only footprints to the top were Eric's. Mine started from nowhere and led nowhere.

Eventually Eric stood up and apologised for his silence, explaining how all the tension of the climb had simply drained from him. He had just wanted to stay there in the snow and let it happen. Both Hannes and I felt an overwhelming relief now the climb was over, but for Eric it was so much more. He had finally proved something to himself that he had wanted to do for so long – and knowing Eric as I do, I know it was just for himself. No hankering after glory.

Almost in a daze I exposed some film on the summit, and then the helicopter returned to collect me for one last spiralling shot, an endless panorama around the top of the Eiger, with Eric just sitting there. He didn't wave his arms in triumph as he had done ten years earlier. He remained still, experiencing an altogether different emotional response. Just being there, on top of the Eiger, was enough.

Then the winch was lowered one last time to collect him. Eric had always said that if he managed to get to the top of the North Face alone, he would walk down the West Flank afterwards. But I persuaded him that there was really very little point. Ten minutes away there would be a bottle of beer, maybe a bottle of champagne. It had all been too much. If Eric was physically tired, he didn't show it, but I was certainly emotionally spent.

On the way back I asked the pilot to fly down the North Face, and it was this that shook Eric back to reality.

'Did I really come up that?' he asked with disbelief, adding, 'If I'd seen it all from here, I don't think I'd have bothered!'

'Perhaps you can now appreciate what it was like for me, watching you all the way up. So how does it feel?'

Eric replied, 'I had a few frights, but that was really to be expected.'

'And inwardly?'

'Contentment, satisfaction and relief.'

'And what now?' I asked.

'I'd like a cup of tea.'

160   *above:* We arrived at the summit almost at the same time
161   *below:* It was difficult to know whose nerves had been the most strained

11
FALLING FREE

If you love something set it free
if it comes back – it is yours,
if it doesn't it never was.

ONE OF THE MOST FRIGHTENING experiences of my childhood was inhaling gas at the dentist's. All my apprehensions, as it turned out, were justified, for the daylight dream that followed involved endless tumbling down a shaft of white light. And as I span, my speed increasing, a high-pitched and constant scream in my head rose to an ear-splitting crescendo. I never did reach the bottom, for a dull pain tugged me back to consciousness. My tooth had gone, the downward plunge had been exchanged for a horizontal swaying – and I hated the dentist.

First experiences of parachuting are not dissimilar. Psychiatrists, I am told, spend more time investigating the motivations of people who throw themselves out of aeroplanes than all the other supposedly high-risk sports put together. It is easy to understand why. No one goes to the edge of a high cliff and peers over without sensing the fear of taking that one further step. Having witnessed the danger, you pull back. To make a parachute descent you have to cross that gap, push your mind through the protective barrier of fear, and step into the void. It is an alien move. Not readily understood. Nor can it be reversed. And it is taken voluntarily.

Mountaineering demands acquired skills, vigilance and stamina, and can be extremely dangerous, yet almost always offers the option of retreat. Hang-gliding and ballooning, too, involve skill and danger, but can be approached gently. First flights are usually short or on a balloon tether; instructors give reassuring advice at the moment of take-off and beyond.

162   My girlfriend Mandy floats gently down through a Florida sunset

No one learns canoeing on the bubbling waters of the Dudh Kosi; no one starts to ski on the giant slalom courses of Europe or America. In almost any sport, you start at the bottom – metaphorically at least – and work up.

There can be no gentle approach, however, to parachuting. No reassuring instructor will hold your hand and say nice things to you as you jump. From that split-second when you depart the plane, you are on your own, with a drop beneath your legs of over 2,000 feet, a wind-blast from the propeller that blankets all but its own sound, and a fear that threatens to tie your stomach into unknown knots.

Fear is a controllable emotion. At least in part. But when the Almighty came to hand out the antidote, it was at random. Some men, some women, cope better than others, yet all are frightened, perhaps terrified, at the prospect of their first jump. There would be something wrong if it were not so. A person lacking in fear ought to be restrained from making parachute jumps. Fear, like pain, alerts you to impending danger. If nothing causes you to be afraid, then why take a parachute at all? Next time you travel in a car along a motorway, imagine the speed at which you would hit a bridge, and then imagine, if you can stomach it, the tremendous forces that would smash your body to pulp. That is what could be at the other end of any parachute jump. That is what the fear is protecting you from. Survival is what it's about. Each time your parachute opens, you cheat the law of gravity. But there are no guarantees for the next time, and you never forget it.

Safely on the ground after your first jump, you might persuade yourself that you enjoyed the whole experience, but it is like banging your head against a wall and then rejoicing when you stop. There is an element of masochism in it somewhere. You have seen death and cheated it. In your blissful relief you forget the terrible apprehension that preceded the jump. Some people mask it with a brittle jokiness, but most first-timers sit anxious and silent in the ascending aircraft, not knowing quite what to expect.

I remember my first descent vividly, remember the plane taking off, all too soon, it seemed, after my training. In no time at all we were on the 'Jump Run'. The command: 'In the door!' didn't seem to apply to me. I was already sitting in the hatchway, my feet trailing somewhere in space trying to reach the ground 2,500 feet below.

'Go!'

I was dead. No. I was alive. A jolt on my harness stopped the horrible tumbling. The plane had gone. Silence took over. There was some strange, pulsating, green organism above me, shielding me from the hurt of falling. And suddenly I was laughing, no longer nervously, but genuinely. The green fields seemed miles below. There was a curve on the horizon. If I had been as tall as I felt, I could easily have reached the ground with my toes. There were cars below, driving along planned roads. But I was free. I could float this way and that without hindrance.

All too soon the ground came up to meet me. Another jolt and I was down – alive – and thoughtful. I couldn't wait then to get back into the air and repeat the strange kaleidoscopic experience, the transcendence from consuming fear to pure elation in microseconds. Parachuting drains from you more energy than sex. It reveals a survival instinct far stronger than the urge to procreate. If you had to put as much concentration and willpower into making love as you do into making a parachute jump, then we human beings would all have joined the dinosaurs long since.

When we were planning our Sudanese ballooning adventure, it had seemed to me necessary to take up parachuting seriously and develop proficiency in its gentle arts – both as an emergency escape route and as a camera platform. Although I had made some seven jumps in previous years, when Eric Jones and I hoped to parachute into Patagonia, it was now a question of starting again from scratch, of progressing beyond being on a 'dope rope', that umbilical cord which opens your parachute on your behalf, until I could master panic and freefall for several seconds before opening.

Early on in my retraining I had one alarming experience when things didn't go at all as they should. I 'exited' the plane in the normal way, but looking up to check as the parachute opened, I saw to my horror that four of the rigging lines were caught over the top of the canopy, which had assumed the ungainly shape of a bra with three boobs! An untimely bonus. The lines were exerting a pressure on the inflated fabric rather like a wire cutting through cheese. First one panel popped, quickly followed by a second. And as I watched, aghast, the third panel blew out as well. I felt as if I was exploding in the sky.

It didn't strike me at first how fast I was plummeting to the ground as some of the canopy was still bearing my weight. But folk on the ground could see all too plainly that I was coming down much faster than was good for me and would surely break my legs, or back, or worse. By the time I realised that the ground was racing up to meet me, it was almost too late to take action. The thing to do instantly was to pull the reserve handle. That's what I had been taught. I pulled. First with my right hand, then, with a certain amount of agitation, with both hands together. Nothing happened. It was jammed. Controlling my panic, I opened the flap

163 'Symbiosis' training over Netheravon

manually, pushed the two pins through the grommets holding the parachute in the pack, and threw out the reserve chute. It opened at about 400 feet and, as it did so, the four lines over the top of my main canopy fell away with the release of pressure. Several spectators had had a nasty fright – to say nothing of the man in the air.

With gentlemanly sensitivity, one young student, who had been filming me with a Super-8 movie camera, stopped when he realised I was, as he thought, for the chop. I later gave him a stern talking-to. He would never make a professional that way, I told him!

Statistics will have you believe that most parachutists experience a 'malfunction' sooner or later. With me, it had come sooner. Safely over it, I was cheered to think that, having got the statistic behind me, I might be spared further misadventures. It certainly proved to me how well the mind works in a crisis. Though it may be wise to avoid unnecessary hazards, I now think that caution should never extend to stifling the urge to undertake potentially dangerous activities. Until you do try, you simply cannot know how you will react – and most people emerge from danger feeling much stronger.

Before long I realised that, given the uncertain nature of English weather, I would never achieve a sufficiently rapid rate of progress to enable me to freefall over the Sahara Desert within a few short months. Something had to be done to speed up the process. Then, one night in the pub, Dave Howerski announced he was off to California for a Christmas parachuting holiday and inquired casually whether I would care to join him. I needed no time for reflection, and immediately said yes. What better place to spend Christmas?

From the moment of landing in San Francisco, it was like stepping into another world. We were whisked away by two of Dave's girlfriends and dunked in their Jacuzzi hot tub. A very pleasurable way in which to soothe away jet lag! Next morning we drove the seventy miles up into the mountains, through the Napa winelands of northern California, to Pope Valley.

I shall never forget that first sight of forty sky-divers, dressed in every conceivable colour and wearing psychedelic helmets with stickers all over them, with an equally gaudy assortment of parachute packs on their backs, laughing and bumping into each other as they clambered up the wooden ladder into the fuselage of a DC-3 aeroplane poised at the end of the runway with both props turning.

The plane thundered down the tarmac, narrowly cleared the trees at the far end, and banked away over the nearby hills. Thirty minutes later it was back, making a pass at 13,000 feet so that sixteen sky-divers could take to the air together. I watched transfixed as those little dots tumbled out of the rear of the plane, scattered across the sky, then quickly swam back together to make intricate patterns like cabaret dancers, before opening their parachutes and drifting to earth like rainbow blossom.

To the unskilled eye, bodies falling through the skies hardly seem to be moving. At the same time, the sky-diver is not conscious of the ground-rush, or the earth coming up to meet him at 120 mph, until he is very low. (By low, I mean less than 2,000 feet from the ground.) From 13,000 feet, the freefall delay is seventy seconds before the parachutist needs to open his chute. In that short time he will have fallen two and a half miles, or more than twice the height of the North Face of the Eiger, the greatest mountain wall in Europe. These Californians were performing dances in the sky while falling three times the height of the Matterhorn, a distance equivalent to twenty Eiffel Towers, one atop the other, or ten World Trade Centers jutting upwards into the sky. Freedom is the feeling it gives you, orgasmic the sensation. It is the nearest man will ever come to flying alone. He can swoop like a hawk, fly to his friends, write snowflake patterns in the sky, then, in a billow of silk, float gently earthwards.

All this, however, I did not appreciate at the time. I had yet to respond to the bubbling excitement of it all. I was still very much an earth person. Indeed, I felt so out of my depth I wanted to turn around there and then and go back to what seemed to me the sanity of England. Dave's enthusiasm, on the other hand, was obviously peaking and he couldn't wait to get in there, get on a plane 'load', and make a dive. Ignoring my delaying tactics, he dragged me off to meet Bill Dause, the Drop Zone Operator.

Bill was known to everyone as Dause Vader, a *Star Wars* nickname he had acquired from his habit of always jumping totally in black – black boots, black jumpsuit, black helmet, black backpack. When his parachute opened, that too had a completely black canopy. Such studied panache made him alien enough to my eyes. He seemed indeed to be courting death as, like a huge, annoyed vampire bat, he buzzed through the skies. It turned out that he had accomplished an astonishing 7,000 jumps in his parachuting career. When you consider that, on a good day, it is possible to make, say, four parachute jumps, and that if this were kept up consistently for a week, that would be a total of twenty-eight, consistently for a year 1,456, it follows that Bill Dause can have done very little else in life than fall out of aeroplanes! He came from Salt Lake City and neither smoked nor drank. In his own words, 'We just sky-dive here!'

Bill thumbed through my log-book and said that I should make a ten-second delay as my first Pope Valley jump. Since my longest delay to date was only two and a half seconds, this seemed, to say the least, radical. The next shock in store for me was that the door of the plane (in England normally open all the time) was closed on take-off and not reopened until we were about to 'exit' on the run-in. Americans enjoy their comfort, but it gave me the fright of my life, when eventually the door was raised, suddenly to hear the 80 mph wind rushing within inches of my right ear.

To become good at something, you need to do it often. It is very important to keep the progression building up steadily at the beginning. I had not fallen from a plane for some weeks and was far too tensed-up to drop for ten seconds. To begin with I pulled the rip-cord handle the same instant that I fell out of the aircraft's door. That was no good.

'Pack up your parachute and back into the plane!' ordered Bill.

Next time I managed to roll over and over. The terror was greater than I could imagine – and my ability to imagine terror vividly is unquestionable.

'Try again!'

So back up to 4,000 feet I went with the patient Bill.

By now, at least I had the first fear barrier of letting go the plane under control, but how was I ever to extend the suspense to ten seconds? There followed the customary couple of involuntary rolls and, after what seemed an eternity, my mental alarm clock told me my ten seconds was up. Horror of horrors! The handle was stuck. Two hands, three further rolls, a final gigantic tug, and I was safe. At last I realised how safe parachuting really is.

Before this incident it had worried me that in a state of blind terror I might become frozen with fear and, as a result, perish. Not so. The panic, far from paralysing you, makes you work at treble speed. Phenomenal strength is suddenly at your disposal when survival becomes paramount. I was going to enjoy parachuting after all!

Four jumps later I achieved a twelve-second delay. Throughout those twelve seconds your speed keeps increasing all the time and you might imagine you would continue to accelerate, second by second, with appalling consequences. It is not so. Practice soon shows that because of the air resistance a terminal velocity is reached at 120 mph. It takes twelve seconds to fall the first thousand feet, then five seconds to fall each subsequent thousand. The speed can only be increased if you dive rather than fall flat-to-earth. 120 mph was quite fast enough for me at present. At this speed the rush of wind is the only sound to be heard. You instinctively sense a mattress of air holding you up. It is like swimming without the sea – or skiing without the slope. You know you are falling but it feels like

164   A three-man Star with the fourth approaching

something else. Could it be you are flying?

It is just as well that a freefalling body does stop accelerating. For if you were to continue gaining speed until falling at 400 or 500 mph, your eyes and mouth would tear apart at the edges, loose limbs would fracture and large joints dislocate. Air would no longer behave as if you could move through it with ease, but act in a hostile and invisible way. It is not possible to get out of an aircraft unaided at speeds in excess of 300 mph. Pilots who eject from planes travelling at high speeds survive only by being encapsulated and hence completely protected from the effect of the air's resistance. Even at relatively slow speeds, it is possible to get into an uncontrollable spin and suffer a 'red-out', that is, a loss of consciousness due to an excess of blood in the head.

Next, I was given a more sophisticated parachute, a Para-Commander, which requires more careful landing. It is designed to enable you to steer more easily where you want to go, though as you approach the ground, you find you are not just coming down vertically, but have a considerable forward speed as well. This necessitates flaring out the canopy just prior to landing. I managed to stall it too soon and, though I landed on my feet, I tripped, fell over backwards and trod on my own thumb, breaking it in two places, right through the joint. An X-ray confirmed the damage and the doctor wanted to insert a steel pin through it to make sure I would keep some mobility in the joint. I didn't fancy a steel or any other kind of pin through it, however. It was *my* thumb, after all, and I opted for a plastic cast. I would take my chance on it recovering properly (which, happily, it did).

As in trendy European skiing resorts, the medics here get used to rather specialised injuries, although the doctor remarked somewhat ruefully that many of his potential customers bypass him altogether and are taken straight to the mortuary. An English jumper had broken his back two weeks earlier, and he was taken to hospital. However, he discharged himself soon afterwards when he realised he couldn't pay the mounting medical bills.

My concern now was how to jump with a plastic cast on my right hand. Unless specially made, all parachutes are designed for a right-handed pull. With this large encumbrance covering not only my thumb but most of my wrist and half of the other fingers as well, it was extremely difficult to release the ripcord. The first time I tried, I could not budge the handle. I started spinning violently. Eventually I managed to get it out, but with my left hand, a technique at which I soon became adept. I suppose it's like making love on top of Everest; you know you can do it but it's harder!

Bill Dause was rather amused that this little Englishman should want to carry on jumping with his hand in a cast, and suggested that it might be a good idea if I opened my parachute higher than usual, to give me extra seconds in case of trouble. With this instruction in mind, I found I was doing ten-second delays from 5,000 feet, and had the chute fully opened at 4,000 feet instead of the normal 2,500. The result was that I tended to float further afield as the parachute would be borne along in the upper winds. The walks back were good exercise.

In Britain it is taboo to jump with any form of broken limb, but here I wasn't the only one jumping with a plaster cast. 'Bullet' Betty Hawkins, a slight, pretty girl with long flowing blonde hair, had been involved in a DC-3 crash some months earlier when the plane had ploughed into a thicket on take-off, spewing out sky-divers. Fortunately nobody was killed but several suffered broken arms and legs, and Betty broke her ankle. With a cast on it she was soon perfecting the art of landing on her one good foot.

At last it was my turn to make a jump from the huge DC-3. Without hesitation, I ran towards the door and dived out. Jumping from a plane which has a slipstream of 120 mph is rather like hitting a soft brick wall, which instantly envelops you, turns you, twists you, then throws you away. It took me some seconds to orientate myself and get the right way up, by which time I could see the DC-3 1,000 feet above, circling around to make another drop. I was delighted and relieved it all worked so well and I landed right next to the target pit.

With my log-book recording fifty-three jumps, Bill Dause, controller of my destiny, decided to push me even further. For my fifty-fourth jump I was to leave the plane with a *square* parachute, a Ram-Air, which gives a forward speed of 25 mph and is far more manoeuvrable. (There is a little ditty which runs, 'Round is sound, but square gets you there' – a maxim borne out by friends of mine who recently flew their 'squares' right across the English Channel, starting at 25,000 feet – with oxygen, of course – and floating almost all the way to Paris, only to be arrested by over-zealous gendarmes for illegal entry!) Landing a square parachute is tricky as you have to cut off almost all your forward speed beforehand. Stall too high and you drop like a stone, flare too late and you crunch in. The knack is to do it at exactly the right moment, allowing you to make a dainty ballet-step down. Sinking down on to my knees, I landed my first square parachute.

Already way ahead of the English progression system, I was now to go to a higher altitude. Bill did not confide this to me beforehand, however. His teaching policy is to give his students only just enough information for their well-being and not enough to confuse them or diminish their self-confidence. Instead of the usual jump out at 6,000 feet, it came as a shock to see the drop zone several miles away with the plane still steadily climbing and my altimeter going up beyond 6,000 feet. Before we were back over Pope Valley we had reached 10,000 feet and I was expected to jump, making a freefall delay of fifty seconds, rather than the twenty I had been prepared for. Quite an advance!

During the next few jumps I learned how to 'fly around' the sky, perform back-loops and turns, and – most important of all – to track, a technique which enables you to go into a dive, rather like a falcon's stoop, in order to separate you from the others in the sky before opening your chute, so ensuring that you do not become entangled with someone else opening theirs.

No longer was I confined to solo drops; it was time to jump with other people and relate to them. This elegant and exhilarating form of parachuting is known rather prosaically as 'relative work'. Dave Howerski's idea was to form a six-man 'star' around me, and with great excitement I watched the others flying in close, though I could see Dave wearing a somewhat apprehensive expression. Knowing the difficulty I

165   *above:* When falling with a cast I had to rely on friends to open my chute

was having pulling the handle out with my hand in a cast, he had briefed me not to pull my own parachute this time. Another sky-diver would link up with me and, at 4,000 feet, pull the ripcord for me. Having been 'pinned' by this other sky-diver, I grew concerned lest he should forget his secondary role of releasing my parachute.

'When are you going to pull the bloody thing?' I yelled in his ear.

He grinned, grabbed the handle and, after a couple more seconds, pulled. I felt the parachute lift off my back and I shot up skywards in relation to the others who were still falling free at 120 mph.

Because everything is relative, it indeed appears as if you are shooting upwards rather than that others are dropping away below you. It becomes difficult to gauge how far they are from the ground. They look as if they will crash into it at any second, when in reality they still have fifteen seconds or so before impact – or 'bounce', as it is more affectionately known.

Next came the piggy-back system, the smallest, most comfortable and streamlined piece of kit available. Both main and reserve parachutes are on your back, one on top of the other. This raises your centre of gravity. You have a tiny parachute called a throw-away, which, as its name implies, you first throw into your slipstream; this then creates sufficient drag to

166   *opposite above:* A pilot chute caught in the door and started to deploy a parachute
167   *below left:* The parachute is by now catching air and starting to drag the parachutist upwards
168   *below right:* With the parachute almost inflated, there was no way anyone could hang on

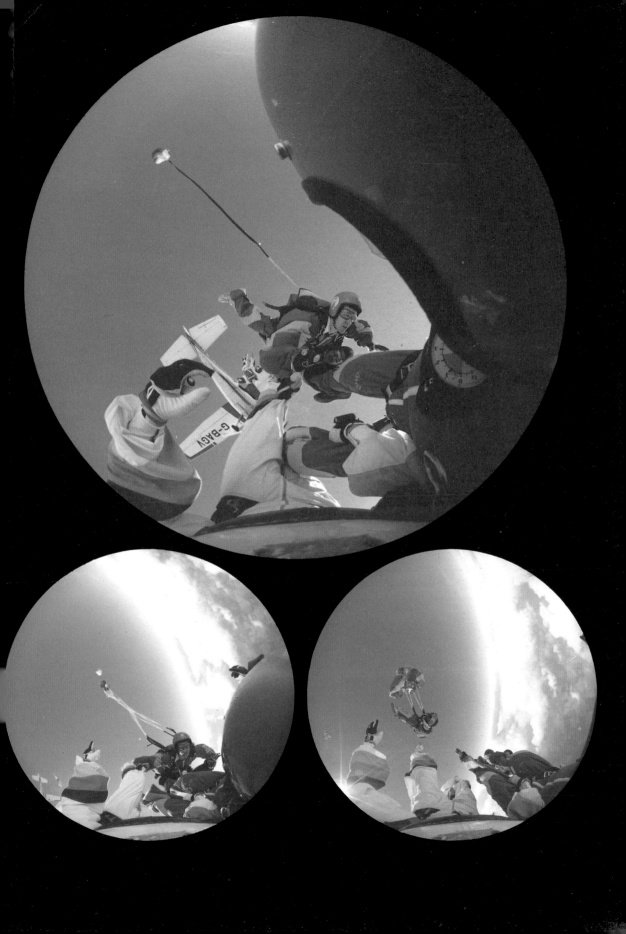

pull the pin opening the main parachute container, thus allowing that to deploy. Unwittingly my camera captured a premature deployment. As five of us fell out of the Cessna simultaneously, the throwaway pilot chute of one of my fellow parachutists caught in the door and opened his backpack. Amazed, he was dragged seemingly upwards as the rest of us fell away from him on our dive. If his chute had not opened properly or had otherwise malfunctioned, he could have pulled the 'single point release pad' on his harness, which would have cut away his main parachute cleanly. Thus no streaming material is left above to tangle around the reserve parachute, which can then be opened.

I was unable to complete the century in Pope Valley because, contrary to popular belief, it rained in California for five days on end. My 100th jump was to be made out of a balloon over the Sahara Desert in the Sudan.

When Dave and I returned from the ballooning expedition, we went back to Pope Valley where, over beautiful green fields and hillsides clothed in colourful spring flowers, several teams were training for the World Parachute Competition to be held in France in August.

The British team of four, called Symbiosis, had as a reserve Jackie Smith, who had been world champion in the accuracy event two years earlier. Jackie had scored ten out of ten dead-centres on the disc, a record never before equalled by man or woman. It is not always realised by the layman, whose mental picture of a sky-diver probably owes much to the daring exploits of the Red Devils, that women make some of the best parachutists. They are often more cool and collected, quicker to learn and more accomplished at manoeuvres, and even suffer less from broken ankles than their heavier counterparts.

Another impressive team busy in Pope Valley was Mirror Image, the American champions. Their name conjures up exactly the view they give from the ground. They are looking-glass people. When they build a formation one way, the person on the ground sees its reflection. The day before last year's championships they screened their *Mirror Image* film for the other competitors. It so demoralised the opposition, seeing this eight-strong team performing up to ten different and perfectly-executed manoeuvres, that the Americans had no trouble in winning the world title!

For the next two weeks I systematically threw myself out of the DC-3, Beechcraft or Cessna, and managed to get in six or seven jumps daily.

169   *above:* High above the English countryside a biplane (left) and a quadroplane (right) fly side by side
170   *below:* An eight-man Star formation high above Pope Valley in California with mists in the background covering San Francisco

Perhaps I grew a little complacent. The importance of split-second timing in formation manoeuvres was brought home to me afresh one evening when making a link-up with a group of four. As they slid beneath me, instead of decelerating by spreading myself 'big' to collect as much air as possible, I put out my hand to fend off the man just below. My little finger caught in his harness and snapped back like a dry twig. I heard a distinct snap, even in the very loud slipstream. I rapidly lost interest in the dive and flew away from the group to get myself out of further difficulties. How was I going to pull out the throw-away pilot chute and open my main canopy with a flopping finger? Fortunately, the incentive to get it open is always there.

Back on the ground, I removed my gloves to inspect the damage. The finger was bent backwards at 90° to the others. The doctor who had treated my thumb at Christmas remembered me and, after several injections and a good deal of wrestling, pulled my finger back into line and taped it to the next one. He told me not to do any more parachuting. But it was no use giving up now and my only concession was to drop back next day from six to three jumps.

The reward for such constancy came from a girl named Cindy. So far I had just bored holes in the air at 120 mph, rather like a super-charged weevil through Camembert. It was Cindy who introduced me to a much more delightful way in which to return from the heavens. Together we went up to 13,000 feet, leapt out of the plane and immediately opened our chutes.

Cindy landed on top of my parachute as we both drifted down, and looked quite happy sitting there with her legs dangling down over the front of my canopy. Why it didn't immediately collapse was a mystery to me, though of course she was supported from above by her own parachute.

'Hang on,' she yelled, 'I'm coming down!' And she promptly hooked her feet around two of my parachute's lines and slid towards me. Surely this was going to collapse my chute, with Cindy standing there on my shoulders. But I had forgotten that Ram-Air parachutes, as the name suggests, take their air not from below, like a round parachute canopy, but from the front, as forward speed rams the air into the canopy's tubular-shaped cells. Separated only by inches, our combined canopies were functioning in perfect harmony, and I began to relax as Cindy piloted us both about the blue Californian sky.

Many more than two can link up in this way, a technique that has

171   *above*: Frank Collins and I forming a biplane
172   *below*: Looking through the top of my parachute at two others attempting to link together

become very sophisticated in recent years and is known as Canopy Relative Work, with world championship displays a testimony to the skill and increasing popularity of the sport. To build a 'stack' or 'plane' requires nerve, precision and complete trust in one's fellow flyers. The stack is started from the top, from where it is piloted, the second chute being steered carefully into the pilot's back so that he can entwine his legs in the second jumper's rigging lines. Beneath this pair a third parachutist prepares for a similar smooth docking, and so on downwards. The dangers of collapsing a canopy through an ill-judged collision, or of becoming entangled in someone else's rigging lines, are ever present. In a stack you are always responsible for the parachutist below you. To escape from an entanglement, it may be necessary to use the quick-release handle, cut away completely and open the reserve chute – if there is time!

I asked Cindy what was the largest formation she had been in. 'Only eight so far,' she replied. Obviously a talented girl since (I later discovered) eight was then the world record.

'Would you like to land this biplane?' Cindy asked.

'If you think I can,' I replied, and touched down a second ahead of her. She landed a few inches in front of me and we rolled over in the long hay of Pope Valley. I got a quick kiss and was totally elated. I little knew then that back in England I would 'dock' thirteenth on a twelve-plane, creating a new world record, and see the film I took on 'News At Ten' the same evening.

It was night-diving that almost put paid to my parachuting enthusiasm for good.

The incident occurred the following Easter in Florida, where 'Forty Tango', the Zephyr Hills C-47, was capable of taking up as many as forty divers at once. The plan was to put together three formations of ten and a couple of smaller ones, leaving four other people to jump out on their own, as it was to be their first night jump. As it happened, there was no moon for the event that had been so carefully organised, but we were all keen to go ahead just the same. After all, the moon is only a bonus. Thousands of military parachutists have made safe night jumps without the help of its shining saucer. All the same, it is very scaring to leap out of an aeroplane into inky blackness. It is rather like committing suicide with your eyes closed. You want to open them, but can't.

I positioned myself next to the door so that I could watch the first ones going out on their way up to 13,000 feet. It would be a good therapy, I told myself. It turned out to be a nightmare.

173   A stack of three over Zephyr Hills

The four soloists were to be dispatched at eight-second intervals to avoid any danger of collision. The first three went out safely, though they appeared to have tumbled unstably into the plane's slipstream. Then it was the turn of Fernando, a Brazilian, a friendly, extrovert young man of whom we had all grown very fond. He left the plane in a perfect spread-eagle position, but hit the blast from the propeller square on. I shall never forget seeing him plucked up like a rag doll and flung backwards into the tailplane.

I could see what was happening ... and yet I couldn't quite see. Impressions and awful premonitions were wrapped up together. Almost immediately we felt a sickening thud and a vibration which shook the whole aircraft. It all happened so fast. I sat dazed with shock, not really sure of all the implications. Seconds afterwards – but already many seconds too late – I thought, 'Should I have dived out ... tried to catch him and open his parachute if he was unconscious?' Later, I was told that to catch an unconscious falling body is virtually impossible. It had been done in daylight, but with near fatal consequences for the catcher. At night, with a body falling erratically, plummeting out of control, it would require a miracle. For me it would have been a fruitless gesture. Poor Fernando was already dead. He had smashed into the back wing at 120 mph and it had almost taken off his head.

It seemed so pointless. Like climbing accidents. Someone remembered all those he had seen killed in Vietnam. Their deaths were senseless too. Fernando was the seventh person he knew who had hit the ground without an open parachute.

You begin to question why you take the risks, but there are no satisfactory answers. To try to justify your motives to others when things go wrong is a self-defeating exercise. Illogical as it may seem, people still go on jumping out of aeroplanes, climbing mountains, and doing all the other things that occasionally kill some of them; few are ever persuaded to give up, even after the shock of witnessing the end of a close companion.

Gradually we went back to parachuting, though we had little heart for it. Until, one spring day, we found a thermal and did not want ever to come down, soaring like birds in the warm air coming up from the hot Florida earth.

Back in England a year later, the tragedy of Fernando already a blurred memory, we tried to put together a 'nonaplane', a nine-man stack, at night over Salisbury Plain. I fitted out each parachutist with a shopwindow-display lamp sunk into a piece of plastic drainpipe, four

174   A quadroplane over Netheravon, with myself second from the bottom

inches long, and powered by lithium sulphur dioxide batteries. As these batteries are said to be at their most efficient below freezing-point, I foresaw no problems in the cold night air. Each drainpiped bulb was then taped to the top of a jumper's helmet.

As we rose over Netheravon airfield, the atmosphere was electric. Edgy voices pretended not to be frightened and cracked jokes that would not have been at all funny at ground-level. Someone accidentally pressed his light switch and the whole plane was suddenly floodlit by a stark beam, surprising expressions of private emotion. We might all have been sitting in a condemned cell.

'Put out that light!' yelled Werner, the pilot. Its harsh glare destroyed his night vision for several minutes.

There was, too, a familiar whiff of gas. Perhaps the lithium batteries were venting, as the manufacturer had warned they might. But no, Mike next to me, with a conspiratorial nudge, indicated it was of human origin. We smirked like schoolboys as the smell was lost to the night air. My brain blanked out the drone of the plane's engines more effectively than ever a man-made silencer could have done.

Soon we were over the drop zone at 10,000 feet. Exit. Within moments the plane might never have existed.

It was very cold. I saw us as nine comets, streaking beneath diamantine skies. Where was I? There was a serenity in the deep silence, and the chill wind was pushing me I knew not where.

The other eight built the first 'octoplane' seen in Britain. I flew around it, filming, absorbing each person's adrenalin as I passed. At 7,000 feet I attempted to dock, but missed. Too fast. Slow down.

Air-traffic controllers ten miles away lost their normally calm, well-modulated accents. 'What the —— is that?' No one had seen such a thing before, an airborne Christmas tree, 100 feet high, blinking in the night air.

As I aimed again, a shadow drifted across my iridescent canopy. A red figure fell through my lines and stopped. We had done it! We had built our 'nonaplane'. We had pocketed a world record. And the camera had recorded scenes the like of which cost Columbia Pictures millions to fake in their *Close Encounters* film.

175–6   *opposite above and below*: Docking on to an octoplane by night and by day; both taken on a helmet-mounted cine camera
177   *main picture*: Canopy Relative Work can go wrong. The combined weight of the two people below was more than No. 6 could hold. The two then fell away tangled together.
177–80   *overleaf top left*: The two span around each other, deflating their parachutes in the process; *middle*: Almost completely-deflated chutes; *below*: The billow of a reserve as the first of the two managed to free himself from the tangled mass of lines and nylon. Fortunately both landed safely.

Acknowledgments

For help in the production of this book I should like to thank Audrey Salkeld, for translating my many tapes and jumbled notes into English, Tony Colwell, our understanding editor at Jonathan Cape, and Brooke Snell, whose design brought the project to a visual reality. But no book of my adventures would have been possible without the adventures themselves and all the friends who accompanied me on them. I am also grateful to the many people who have helped me with my expeditions and filming over the years. It is a long list.

There are Bob and Ellis Brigham, who gave me so much early encouragement; Ian and Jan Phillips who have coped superbly with my sometimes highly ambitious technical requirements; Roger Goodwill and Ted Grey of Blackpool School of Art; Ian McNaught Davis for his humorous film scripts; all my colleagues at HTV Wales – in particular Aled Vaughan, Huw Davies and Colin Voisey – Terry Elgar, Dave Camps, John Cross, Viv Grant and also Chris Grace, Filip Cieslik, Norman Cunningham, Geraint Rees, Mike Reynolds and Bob Stokes; Michael Deakin, Barry Reynolds and the late Tony Essex of Yorkshire Television; Richard Creasey, Glen Cardno, Bryony Coombe, Roger James, June Peacock, Noel Smart and Mark Anstiss of ATV; Pete Hutchinson of Mountain Equipment; Mike Parsons and Eddie Creig of Karrimor International; Denny Moorhouse of Clog; Ron Collins, George Hill and Geoff Chapell of Optical and Textile; Ems Magnus, Brian Hall, Ray Peake and Ron Thorn of Canon; David Payne and David Dearden of ICI; Constant Cachin, Albert Kunz, Josef Luggen and Jorge Schmidt of the Swiss Tourist Offices; Ernest Schudel of Photo-Suisse in Grindelwald; and Brian Morgan of Warwick Productions.

Then also I should like to thank all my parachuting colleagues: Steve Anderson, Gary Carter, Dave Cooper, Bill Dause, Rande Deluce, Jim Hooper, Dave Howerski, Jordie Laing, Charlie Shea-Simmonds and all the Mounting Men; also balloonists Don Cameron, Bob Kenny and Alan Noble.

I acknowledge help also from Chris Brasher, Ronald Faux, Casimiro Ferrari, Peter Gillman, George Greenfield, Lisa van Gruisen and Liz Hawley of Kathmandu, Allen Heap, Pedro Korzhenewsky, Cesare Maestri, John Pugsley, Dr Eduardo Rodriguez, Martin Schliessler and Ian Skipper.

The extract on pages 206–7, from a review first published in the *Observer*, appears in the collection *The Crystal Bucket* by Clive James (Cape, 1981), and is reprinted by kind permission of the author.

Finally, but by no means least, my thanks go to my brother, Donald Dickinson, and my close friend and co-adventurer Eric Jones.

PICTURE CREDITS

With the exception of those listed below all photographs were taken by myself. My thanks are due to the following:

Maggie Cameron: 5, 10; Glen Cardno: 11; Mick Coffey: 59; Arthur Gibson: 174; Peter Habeler: 147; Rob Hastings: 81; Dave Howerski: frontispiece, 104, 112, 115, 165, 171; Eric Jones: 3, 22, 33, 34, 77, 80, 83, 120, 128; John Liddle: 92; Barbara Lloyd: 88, 90; Reinhold Messner: 146; Peter Minks: 26; *Mountain* magazine archive: 43; Robert Schauer: 129; Brian Smart: 2; Hannes Stähli: 161; Hans Peter Trachsel: 41, 44.

getting close-up shots of the final assault on the summit was to give Messner himself the camera and hope that he would be able to cope.

The enormously long, almost obscene, 1200 mm telephoto lens I used can be seen in plate 129, in which I am filming some action on the Lhotse Face a couple of miles away. In plate 142 Sherpas can be seen through this lens leaving Camp III. The more modest 100 mm macro-lens provided the shot of Dawa Tensing in plate 130. A 20 mm wide-angle lens was used to film through the crevasse ladder in plate 135 to the cavern below, and also for the picture of Camp II in plates 140 and 141.

Flash helped the fading daylight for plate 144, showing the doctors attending the stricken Sherpa, and plate 130 was achieved by leaving the camera on its tripod with the shutter open while I moved from tent to tent giving each in turn a quick burst from my flash gun.

Plate 146, showing Peter Habeler nearing the summit, was taken with a 35 mm lens on the Canon AE1, which I had left on automatic exposure before handing it over to Reinhold Messner. The cine camera which Messner took to the top was the little Canon 310XL Super-8 also set on automatic exposure, which suffered slightly by the exposure meter iris becoming choked with spindrift. It can be seen at the bottom of plate 147.

10 THE SPIDER AND THE FLY

During the five years in which Eric toyed with the idea of a solo ascent of the Eiger I constantly revised my filming plans should it ever become reality.

The helicopter trip to Death Bivouac necessitated minimal equipment. I took my Canon A1 with 35–70 mm zoom as well as the 300 mm. For the Beaulieu I used a 5.7 mm wide-angle, the Canon 10:1 zoom and the same 300 mm as used for stills. On the more friendly West Flank a heavier Sachtler 7+7 tripod to steady the Canon 800 mm telephoto that brought the Traverse of the Gods so close was used.

Plates 155, 158, 159 and 160 were all taken from the helicopter on the 35–70 mm zoom.

11 FALLING FREE

It is impossible to operate a camera by hand while in freefall, and it is best to have it mounted on top of your helmet, whether it be stills or cine. A remote release is necessary to trigger the camera and a sight parallel to the lens is placed in front of one eye. Wide-angle and fisheye lenses work best, using a shutter speed of at least a two-hundred-and-fiftieth of a second. A motordrive is almost as important as your parachute. You are falling at 120 mph and expecting to operate a camera.

Plates 164 and 170 were taken on a 24 mm wide-angle. The sequence of plates 166–8 was taken on a 7.5 mm fisheye lens. Plate 172 was on a 15 mm fisheye lens.

Canopy Relative Work is slower and a hand-held camera is preferable for more accurate framing.

The little electrically-driven Bell and Howell protected in its underwater housing (plate 80) and mounted on the front of the canoe was responsible for plate 79. A low evening sun lit plate 78 and a flash gun was held ten feet to the side of the cooks in plate 83. Stills of the canoeists were covered by my Canon F1 with a five-frame-per-second motordrive (plates 85 and 89). Many frames were discarded because the canoe was underwater as it passed the camera.

Plate 87, showing the South Face of Lhotse, with monsoon clouds swirling below, was taken with a 300 mm lens to isolate the mountain from its neighbours. Two cameras, one with a zoom lens and one with a wide-angle lens, were taped together to film the canoeists going down the gorge where Mick Hopkinson nearly drowned (plate 92). The sequence of plates 95–102 was taken at the extreme end of the 120 mm zoom range, from the HTV film. It was often difficult to see Mike Jones and even more difficult to see the bobbing head of Hoppy through the viewfinder as they were swept downstream. Plate 44 was the only 35 mm still of this incident.

7 DIVING INTO THE SAHARA

The heat of the Sahara can be just as trying as the cold of Everest and the dry dusty air equally cruel to a camera as insidious cold. Polythene bags kept at least some of the grit away but I did have more camera failures on this trip than on any other.

In the proximity of a balloon basket wide-angle lenses are most useful for filming the inhabitants; the 20 mm wide-angle was used on plates 105, 106, 107 and the 15 mm fisheye on plates 111 and 116.

Dave Howerski and I filmed each other with two modified Autoloads mounted on our helmets for plate 104, and for plate 109 a tripod was mounted horizontally on to the basket to take the Beaulieu with the 3.5 mm fisheye lens.

Plates 114 and 115 show two 'perfect' camera platforms and it was from the latter that I filmed Dave's jump and subsequent docking back on to the balloon (plates 117, 118 and 119).

8 DHAULAGIRI, WHITE GODDESS

Although this was only a small expedition, there still seemed to be an immense amount of luggage to transport. The back-lighting effect caused by mist in plate 123 provides an interesting picture of our preparations. For all pre-dawn pictures – for example, plate 121 – it was almost impossible to get an exposure reading. Inevitably there is more light around than the meter would have you believe. Later, on the way up to Camp I at 16,000 feet, I travelled light, with only the small Bell and Howell cine camera.

It is worth noting that the exposure for plate 122 had to be for the snow highlights. A slow shutter speed gave a lovely quality to plate 126.

9 EVEREST WITHOUT OXYGEN

Filming at a distance through a zoom or telephoto lens requires a firm tripod, otherwise the smoothest pans appear jerky and the steadiest hand gives an impression on the screen of a high wind buffeting the camera. On Everest, a good deal of the action has to be recorded in this way from afar. The only chance of

side of the valley to Cerro Torre. The cramped ice-cave seen in plate 41 was taken by flash.

4 LAND OF MIST AND FIRE

Never have I found it so easy, or rewarding, to photograph wildlife as I did in Patagonia. The almost tame fox in plate 51 and the torrent duck in plate 52 were both taken with a 300 mm telephoto lens. The pygmy owl in plate 53 was captured by flash.

Flash was also used for the photograph of the inside of our four-by-six-foot Bokz tent, seen in plate 55, as well as for plate 60 as we prepared in the dark for an early-morning start.

The 17 mm lens was used to take plates 54, 55, 58, 62, 65, and 64 using the self-timer. Being such a wide-angle lens it gave a feeling of immense open spaces which suited this location admirably.

It was in South America that I learned never to be afraid of strong back light for interesting mountain photographs.

5 IN THE FOOTSTEPS OF EDWARD WHYMPER

Nowhere have I encountered less favourable conditions for photography (not to mention climbing) than on the Matterhorn in winter. But it is no good just putting the cameras away because of poor light, dense cloud or seemingly impenetrable spindrift. Such adversities will often yield the most dramatic effects.

Our reconstruction of the Edward Whymper tragedy was not completed without its own moments of drama. Eric's spectacular 100-foot fall down a steep snow slope was recorded (plate 69) only because I happened to have the Canon Scoopic running when it occurred. It was a near thing, and we little knew then that it was to be the first of a series of agonising moments.

The winter view of the mountain through a 50 mm lens in plate 67 does nothing to portend the awfulness of the night we were to spend on a rocky perch barely big enough to stand, let alone sleep, on (plate 73). On a bivouac ledge the 20 mm wide-angle lens gives a feeling of involvement, but does not give a true perspective in plate 71 of the angle of the great ice sheet on the North Face, which is more apparent in plate 72.

Plate 75, taken on a 35 mm lens, and plate 76, a blow-up from the 16 mm film taken on the Canon Scoopic, show what you can get on film in impossible conditions during the worst storm this century in the Zermatt region.

6 CANOEING DOWN THE ROOF OF THE WORLD

Technically the film taken on the Dudh Kosi river was far more advanced and experimental than the earlier ones, and its success is reflected by the twenty awards gained by the final result.

Some idea of our approach to filming on fast white water may be gained from the main body of text. I would always set up the shore-based cameras downstream from the canoeists, indicate I was ready and wait for the unexpected to happen. So fast was the river flow that I rarely saw a canoeist for more than twenty seconds as he sped past me.

cine camera similarly suspended was operated by an ultrasonic control unit held in my hand. Plate 9 was taken through the 15 mm fisheye lens inside the balloon envelope itself. Plate 10 shows the Photosonic IVN camera attached to my helmet. Plate 12 was taken with a 15 mm fisheye lens just before I jumped out at 15,000 feet; 13 is from the 16 mm ATV film. Because of the extreme cold at altitude, the cameras were wrapped in foam rubber and the batteries placed inside Thermos flasks.

Similar techniques were employed for Don Cameron's baby experimental balloon. One cine camera was attached to the balloon envelope pointing downwards, one to the upright of the basket pointing vertically upwards, and the third secured to the parachuting helmet on my head. The sequence in plates 16–19 is made up from 16 mm frames from these cameras. The first picture shows the bottom part of the balloon being sucked into the top. The second was taken looking down at me in the basket before the experiment began to go wrong, and the third and fourth from the same position as I was flung from the basket. The violent spinning threw the ground below into a blur as I fell away, 300 feet below, where it was safe to open my parachute.

2 THE EIGER EXPERIMENT

The hazards of filming the ascent of the Eiger North Wall were not confined to extending the climb over several days. The encumbrance of cameras and film stock in our backpacks restricted our movements and tired us out. There is little room for a tripod on the North Face and all the filming had to be accomplished with hand-held cameras. Looking through the viewfinder in exposed positions can be disorientating. Loading film into the camera on a 60° slope is extremely difficult, to say nothing of filming while tip-toeing on front points of crampons dug a mere fraction of an inch into the ice.

On early sections we climbed as two ropes of two for greater filming flexibility and in an attempt to speed up our rate of progress. Most of the filming on this expedition was done with the Canon Scoopic. The sequence in plates 23–5 of Cliff Phillips's spectacular fall is taken from the final edited 16 mm Yorkshire TV film. The central section of the North Wall shown in plate 21 was taken with a Canon F1 and a 100 mm lens from Mannlichen a couple of miles from the Eiger. The remaining photos were taken on standard lenses.

3 CERRO TORRE

Photography in the region of Cerro Torre in the Andes requires patience and opportunism. So vast in scale are the landscapes that one also needs a good range of lenses in order to be ready to catch the extraordinary effects of light with the sudden breaks in the prevailing cloud.

Plates 36 and 38 show the heavy ice formations that attach themselves to the last 800 feet of the Headwall, taken with a Canon 1200 mm lens from a distance of about five miles shortly after a storm. Plate 45, showing Cerro Torre, was given a four-minute time exposure when the mountain was bathed in moonlight reflected from the glacier. The thin streaks indicate the movements of stars and the brighter streak the path of the planet Venus. The 17 mm Canon super wide-angle lens was used for the breathtaking view (plate 48) seen from the opposite

Appendix: NOTES ON PHOTOGRAPHY

The photographic content of this book falls into two categories: those photographs which were taken directly on 35 mm still cameras and those which are from 16 mm film sections. For stills I used Canon bodies F1, AE1 and A1 with the following lenses: 7.5 and 15 mm fisheye; 17 and 20 mm super wide-angle; 24 and 35 mm wide-angle; 35–70 mm zoom; 50 and 100 mm macro; 300, 600, 800 and 1200 mm telephoto. A Canon two-times extender was also occasionally useful.

The flash units were Speedlights and the motordrives MD, MF and Power-winders. A wire-less Controller LC1 (remote control unit) was used to trigger the A1, and the 16 mm frames were copied using a Canon 35 mm macro-photo lens with 16 mm duplicator.

The 16 mm cine cameras were Canon Scoopic, Bell and Howell DR70, Bell and Howell Autoloads, Beaulieu R16, Photosonic IVN and Aaton 7–LTR. Apart from the Scoopic, all the cine camera bodies took either C-mount lenses or Canon 35 mm lenses. The Beaulieu was modified to take both. My Canon telephoto lenses could therefore be fitted to 35 mm still cameras as well as to the Beaulieu and Aaton 16 mm. Other lenses used for filming were: Century 3.5 mm fisheye; Century 5.7 mm wide-angle; Angenieux 10 mm, 25 mm, 50 mm. The zoom lens I used was the Canon Macro-Fluorite 12–120 mm. Two Bell and Howell Autoloads were modified to run electrically and the shutters changed to enable them to take a Canon 6 mm VTR lens, which was used extensively on the Dudh Kosi expedition.

For stills I used Kodachrome 25 or 64 and Agfa CT18, and for 16 mm movies Kodak Eastmancolour negative 7247.

LIGHT READINGS

Expeditions are compromises in many ways, not least in photography. Most still, and indeed many cine, cameras these days have 'through the lens metering'. This is often the most convenient way of measuring light but should be used with care. Large areas of light, such as snow, will tend towards underexposure, just as large dark areas, such as forests, will tend towards overexposure.

There is no real substitute for an incident light-meter reading in the subject area, but if this is several thousand feet above your head, then a telephoto lens mounted on a 'through the lens metered' camera saves making this climb!

1 THE GREAT BALLOON RACE

The secret of successful filming on any balloon flight lies in careful placement of cameras, there being no vibration in the structure itself. Some of the most dramatic pictures of Julian Nott's attempt on the altitude record were taken on the Canon A1 with motordrive, suspended from the widest part of the balloon envelope about twenty-five feet away from the gondola. The Photosonic IVN

When we landed, our bodies were plied with drinks, but our brains were already highly intoxicated. The film was duly dispatched to ITN's 'News At Ten', but they were unable to make head or tail of what we were supposed to be doing. That night Ronald Reagan was shot on the world's TV screens – an altogether more comprehensible happening. Martians could have landed that day and, like us, no doubt, would have been nudged from the headlines!

Over the Easter holiday we tried again, this time with sixteen people, requiring two planes and a complicated run-in sequence. The atmosphere inside the aircraft was as tense as before. This time I had taped a camera and light to the outside of the Islander to record our exit. The beam stabbed the darkness for fifty feet, then ended.

We fell out simultaneously, the other Islander dropping its human cargo fifty feet to our left. The camera faithfully recorded the nine of us falling into oblivion. The full moon dulled our senses. It was light up there above the earth, but all below was dark.

An eight-parachute stack was built, but then things began to go horribly wrong. Parachutes three and four started to oscillate, swinging wildly in opposite directions until they blew the stack apart backwards. Two went down spinning, tangled together in reluctant combat. One managed to cut away after a while and open his reserve. He was safe. But the second spun on earthwards for minute-long seconds before he was able to get his reserve open and cut away – a strange order but he, too, was safe. The earth sucked us all down.

The next day my car was due to be serviced and the garage sent round an old man to collect it. I invited him in and he noticed a parachute photograph on the wall – a four-stack over cloud. His eyes cleared as he asked me if I was in the photo.

'Yes,' I admitted, adding, 'in fact, yesterday we did a tremendous night jump. A nineplane. And I filmed it with lights.' I didn't expect him to understand.

'I did a parachute jump at night once,' he volunteered. 'Out of a Lancaster. We had lights too – the fuel tanks exploded and 2,000 gallons of petrol caught alight!'

Numbed, I asked if he had done many jumps.

'Only the one,' was the reply.